The Shubert Organization and Emanuel Azenberg
by arrangement with
Playwrights Horizons
present

C000091259

SUNDAY in the PARK with GEORGE

A Musical

Music and Lyrics by
Stephen Sondheim

Book by
James Lapine

with

Mandy Patinkin   Bernadette Peters

Charles Kimbrough   Barbara Bryne   Dana Ivey

Mary D'Arcy   Danielle Ferland   Cris Groenendaal
Kurt Knudson   Judith Moore   Nancy Opel
William Parry   Brent Spiner   Melanie Vaughan
and Robert Westenberg

Scenery by   Costumes by   Lighting by
Tony Straiges   Patricia Zipprodt and Ann Hould-Ward   Richard Nelson

Special Effects by   Sound by   Hair and Makeup   Movement by
Bran Ferren   Tom Morse   Lo Presto/Allen   Randolyn Zinn

Musical Direction by   Orchestrations by   Music Published by
Paul Gemignani   Michael Starobin   Tommy Valando

Directed by
James Lapine

Live dramatic performance rights for "Sunday in the Park with George" are represented exclusively by
Music Theatre International (MTI)
421 West 54th Street, New York, NY 10019.
www.MTIshows.com
For further information, please call (212) 541-4684
or email: Licensing@MTIshows.com.

ISBN 978-1-4234-7271-1

RILTING MUSIC, INC.

EXCLUSIVELY DISTRIBUTED BY

7777 W. BLUEMOUND RD. P.O. BOX 13819 MILWAUKEE, WI 53213

Visit Hal Leonard Online at
www.halleonard.com

SUNDAY IN THE PARK WITH GEORGE opened at the
Booth Theatre in New York on May 2, 1984

ORIGINAL CAST
Act I

GEORGE, an artist .... Mandy Patinkin
DOT, his mistress .... Bernadette Peters
an OLD LADY .... Barbara Bryne
her NURSE .... Judith Moore
FRANZ, a servant .... Brent Spiner
a BOY bathing in the river .... Danielle Ferland
a YOUNG MAN sitting on the bank .... Nancy Opel
a MAN lying on the bank .... Cris Groenendaal
JULES, another artist .... Charles Kimbrough
YVONNE, his wife .... Dana Ivey
a BOATMAN .... William Parry
CELESTE #1 .... Melanie Vaughan
CELESTE #2 .... Mary D'Arcy
LOUISE, daughter of Jules and Yvonne .... Danielle Ferland
FRIEDA, a cook .... Nancy Opel
LOUIS, a baker .... Cris Groenendaal
a SOLDIER .... Robert Westenberg
a MAN with a bicycle .... John Jellison
a LITTLE GIRL .... Michele Rigan
a WOMAN with a baby carriage .... Sue Anne Gershenson
MR. .... Kurt Knudson
MRS. .... Judith Moore

Act II

GEORGE, an artist .... Mandy Patinkin
MARIE, his grandmother .... Bernadette Peters
DENNIS, a technician .... Brent Spiner
BOB GREENBERG, the museum director .... Charles Kimbrough
NAOMI EISNER, a composer .... Dana Ivey
HARRIET PAWLING, a patron of the arts .... Judith Moore
BILLY WEBSTER, her friend .... Cris Groenendaal
a PHOTOGRAPHER .... Sue Anne Gershenson
a MUSEUM ASSISTANT .... John Jellison
CHARLES REDMOND, a visiting curator .... William Parry
ALEX, an artist .... Robert Westenberg
BETTY, an artist .... Nancy Opel
LEE RANDOLPH, the museum's publicist .... Kurt Knudson
BLAIR DANIELS, an art critic .... Barbara Bryne
a WAITRESS .... Melanie Vaughan
ELAINE .... Mary D'Arcy

Act I takes place on a series of Sundays from 1884 to 1886 and alternates
between a park on an island in the Seine just outside of Paris, and George's
studio.

Act II takes place in 1984 at an American art museum and on the island.

MUSICAL NUMBERS

ACT ONE   PAGE

Opening Prelude 1
Flying Trees...3
Sunday In The Park With George 3
Parasol 16
Yoo-Hoo! 17
No Life...18
Scene Change To Studio 23
Color And Light 24
Scene Change To Park 48
Gossip Sequence..50
Cues In The Park 57
The Day Off 57
Everybody Loves Louis 80
The One On The Left 90
Finishing The Hat 94
Bustle 102
Scene Change To Studio 104
We Do Not Belong Together...105
Beautiful 116
Soldier Cue #1 124
Jules and Frieda 125
Soldier Cues #2 and #3 125
Chaos 126
Sunday..126

ACT TWO

It's Hot Up Here...135
Eulogies 147
Chromolume #7 (Part I) 150
Chromolume #7 (Part II) 151
Putting It Together..157
Children And Art 204
After Children 212
Lesson #8 213
Move On..219
Sunday - Finale 234
Bows 239
Exit Music...245

INSTRUMENTATION

Reed 1: Flute, Clarinet, Bass Clarinet, English Horn, Piccolo, Soprano Sax
Reed 2: Flute, Oboe, Clarinet, English Horn, Piccolo, Alto Sax

Horn (B-flat & F)

Percussion
Piano/Celeste
Harp
Synthesizer

Violin 1
Violin 2
Viola
Cello

This score has been prepared from the composer's piano manuscript rather than the piano-conductor score so that it can be more useful to the rehearsal pianist. As a result, when the orchestral parts are utilized, some small musical discrepancies will be found. Insofar as discrepancies in the lyrics are concerned, this vocal score is to be considered correct.

Vocal Score prepared by PAUL McKIBBINS

The composer wishes to express his thanks to Paul Ford and Theodore Sperling for their assistance in the preparation of this score and to Michael Starobin for his arrangement of the themes for the musical effects in *Chromolume #7*.

Music typography by David M. Carp.

for Jim, with love and thanks

SUNDAY IN THE PARK WITH GEORGE
ACT I

No. 1 ### OPENING PRELUDE

A white stage. White floor, slightly raked and extended in perspective.
Four white portals define the space. The proscenium arch continues
across the bottom as well, creating a complete frame around the stage.

George enters Downstage. He is an artist. Tall, dark beard, wearing a
soft felt hat with a very narrow brim crushed down at the neck, and
a short jacket. He looks rather intense. He sits Downstage on the
apron at an easel with a large drawing pad and a box of chalk. He stares
momentarily at the pad before turning to the audience.

Music and Lyrics by
STEPHEN SONDHEIM

GEORGE: White. A blank page or canvas.
The challenge: bring order to the whole.
(A tree flies in Stage Right)

Through design.

*(The white portals fly out and the white ground cloth
comes off, revealing a grassy-green expanse and portals
depicting a park scene)*

Composition. *(Two trees descend)*

Balance. *(A tree tracks on from Stage Left)*

Light.

*(The lighting bumps, giving the
impression of an early morning
sunrise on the island of "La
Grande Jatte" - - harsh shadows
and streaming golden light
through the trees)*

GEORGE *(cont'd):* And harmony.

(George goes to the wings and escorts Dot towards the

audience. She wears a traditional 19th century outfit: full length dress with bustle, etc. When he gets her

Downstage Left, he turns her profile, then returns Downstage to his easel. He begins to draw. She turns to him)

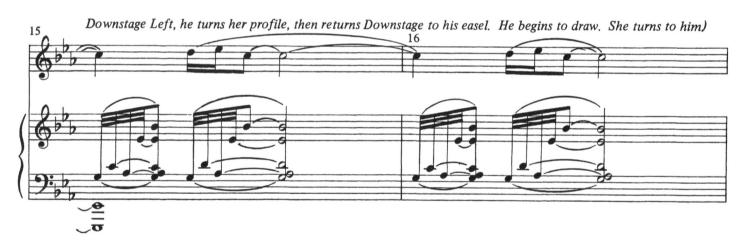

GEORGE:	*(Annoyed)* No. Now I want you to look out at the water.	DOT.	Why wear it? Everyone is wearing them!
DOT:	I feel foolish.	GEORGE.	*(Begins sketching)* Everyone...
GEORGE:	Why?	DOT:	You know they are. *(She begins to move)*
DOT:	*(Indicating bustle)* I hate this thing.		
GEORGE:	Then why wear it?	GEORGE:	Stand still, please.

Repeat, gradually fading out under the above dialogue; out by George's last line.

No. 2   FLYING TREES

DOT: What's the matter?

GEORGE: *(Erasing feverishly)* I hate this tree. *(A tree rises back into the flies)*

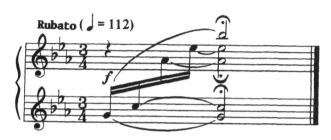

No. 3   SUNDAY IN THE PARK WITH GEORGE
(DOT)

GEORGE: More boats. *(Tugboat appears)* More trees. *(More trees track on)*   DOT: George.

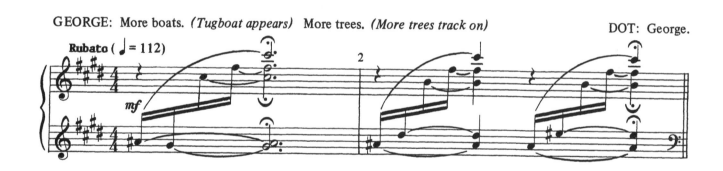

Why do you always get to
sit in the shade while I have
to stand in the sun? *(No response)*   George? *(Still no response)*   There is someone in this
Hello, George?   dress! *(Twitches slightly)*

4

5

8

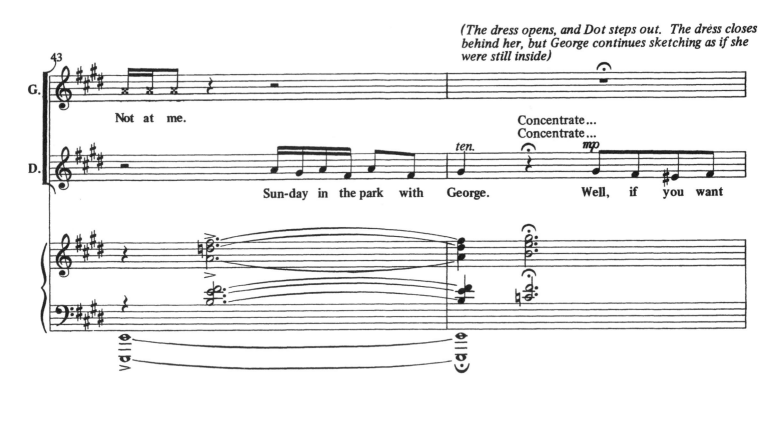

(The dress opens, and Dot steps out. The dress closes behind her, but George continues sketching as if she were still inside)

G. Not at me.

D. Sun-day in the park with George.

Concentrate...
Concentrate...

Well, if you want

D. bread And re-spect And at - ten - tion, Not to say con - nec - tion, Mod-el-ling's no pro -

mp leggiero

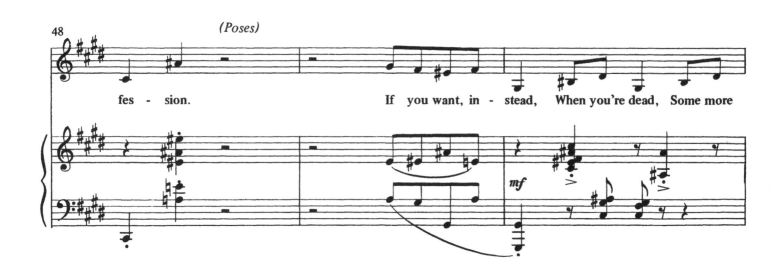

(Poses)

fes - sion.   If you want, in - stead,   When you're dead,   Some more

mf

No. 4 PARASOL

OLD LADY: Hand me my parasol.

NURSE: I am, Madame.

No. 5

YOO-HOO!

OLD LADY: ... What is all that commotion?

FRANZ: Jungen! Nicht so

(A wagon tracks on, showing a likeness of "Une Baignade Asnieres")

laut! Ruhe, bitte!   BOY: Yoo-hoo! Dumb and fat!   YOUNG MAN: Hey! Who you staring at?

PERVERT: Look at the lady with the rear! *(The Young Man gives a loud Bronx cheer)*   BOY: Yoo-hoo -- kinky beard!

PERVERT: Kinky beard!   YOUNG MAN, BOY: Kinky beard!   *(George gestures -- all freeze. A frame comes in around them. Segue immediately)*

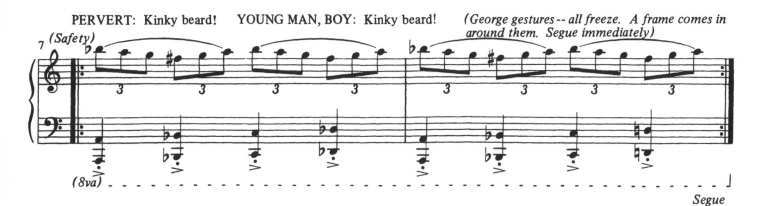

Segue

No. 6

NO LIFE
(JULES, YVONNE)

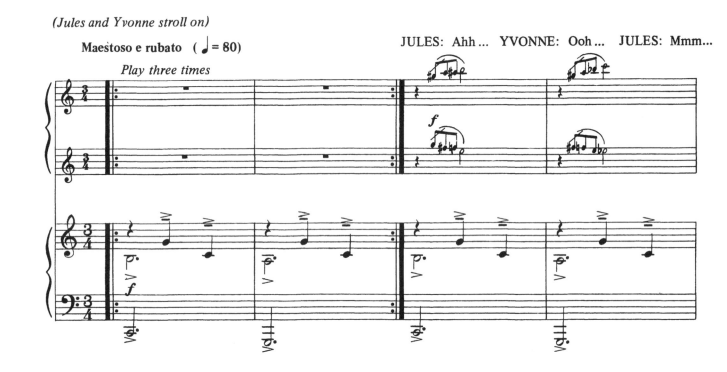

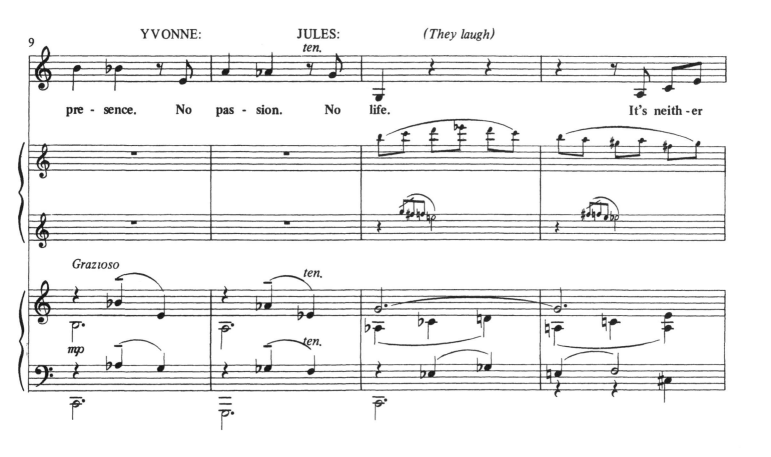

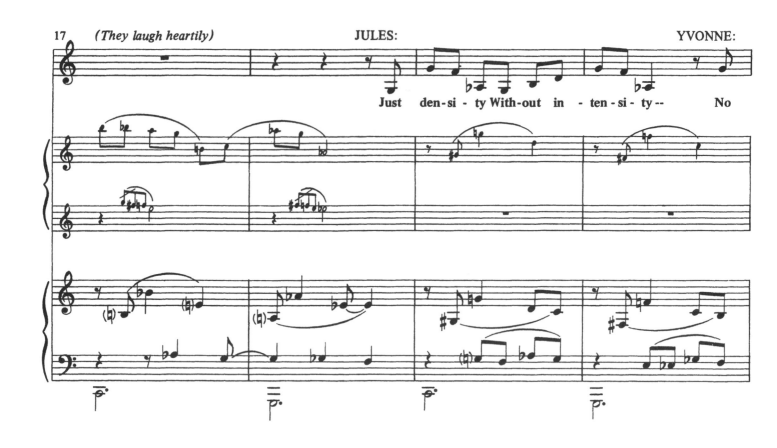

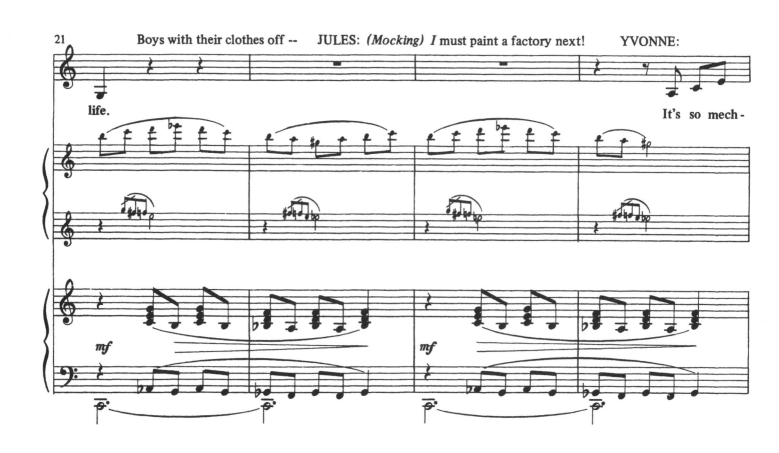

No. 7   SCENE CHANGE TO STUDIO

OLD LADY: Some other day, Monsieur.

GEORGE: It's George, Mother.

OLD LADY: *(As if it is to be a secret)* Sssh ...

GEORGE: *(Exiting)* Yes. I guess we will all be back.

No. 8

COLOR AND LIGHT (Part I)
(DOT, GEORGE)

*George's studio. Upstage, hidden at first, he stands on a
scaffold, behind a large canvas, which is a scrim. He is
painting. Downstage, Dot (in a likeness of "La Poudreuse")
is at her vanity, powdering her face.*

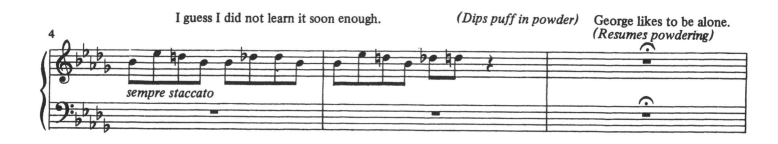

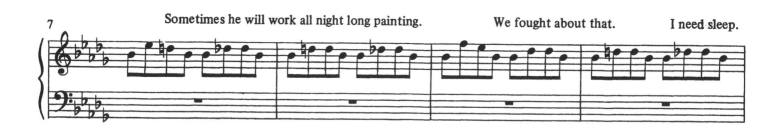

26

56

G.

col-or and light.

Yel-low and white.

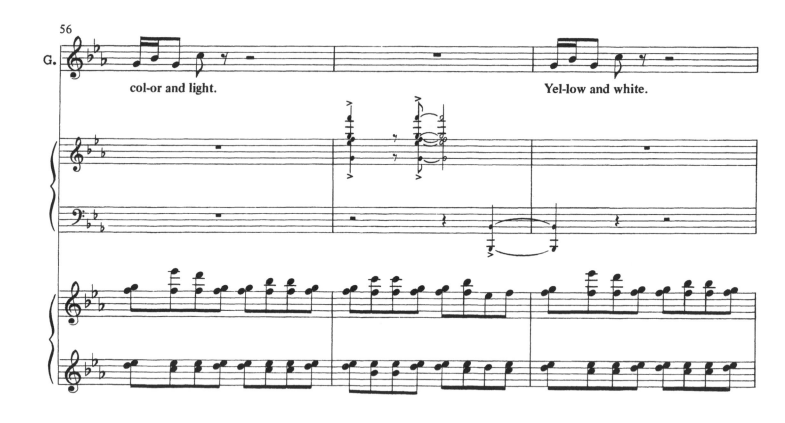

59

(Addressing the woman he is painting)

Just blue and yel-low and white.

Look at the air, Miss-- See what I mean?

No, look ov-er there, Miss-- That's done with

(Swirling a brush in the orange cup)

green ... _____ Con - joined with or-ange ...

Segue

No. 8A   **COLOR AND LIGHT (Part II)**
(DOT, GEORGE)

*(Lights down on George, up on Dot,
now powdering her breasts and armpits)*

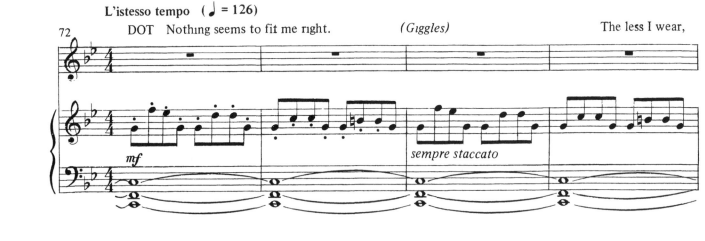

L'istesso tempo (♩ = 126)

DOT Nothing seems to fit me right.   *(Giggles)*   The less I wear,

sempre staccato

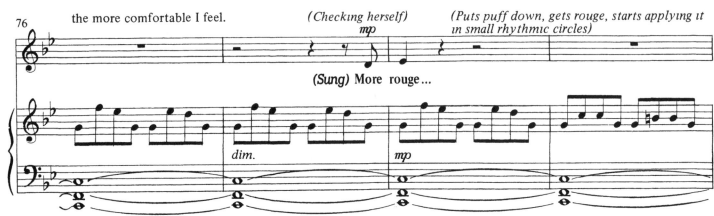

the more comfortable I feel.   *(Checking herself)*   *(Puts puff down, gets rouge, starts applying it
in small rhythmic circles)*

(Sung) More rouge...

dim.

32

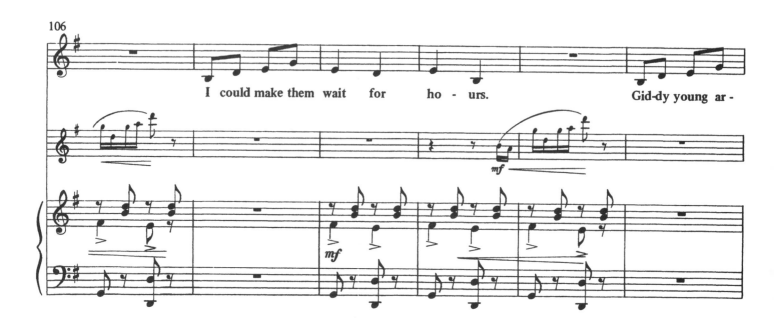

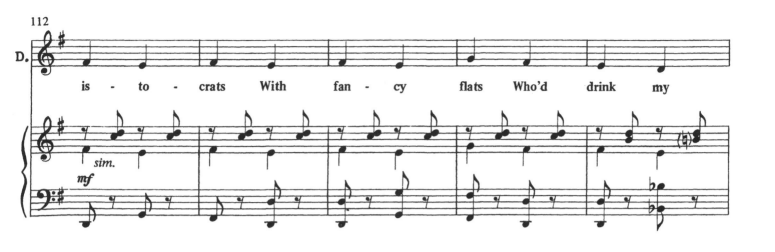

is - to - crats With fan - cy flats Who'd drink my

(Looks at her nails, reaches for the buffer)

health, And I would be as hard as nails ...

(Buffs nails rhythmically)   *poco rall.*

And they'd on - ly want me more ... If I was a

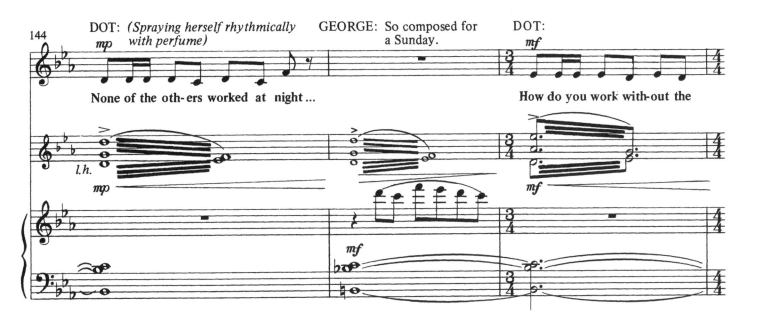

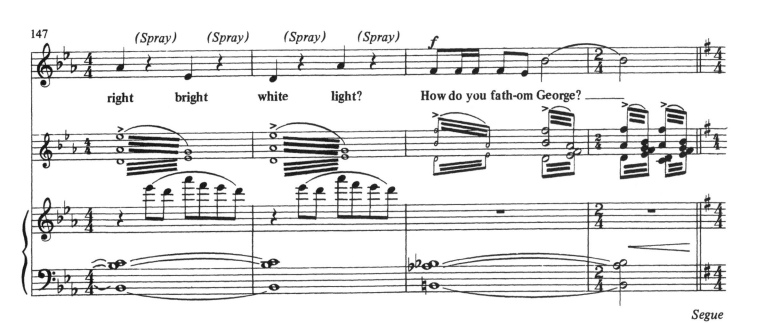

Segue

No. 8B   COLOR AND LIGHT (Part III)
(DOT, GEORGE)

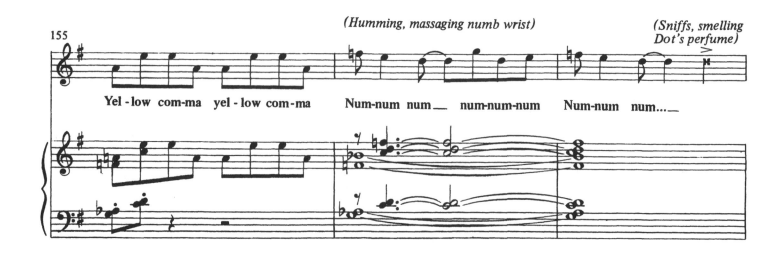

* *Optional in Bars 168 and 169· this voice may be either whistled or played in the orchestra.*

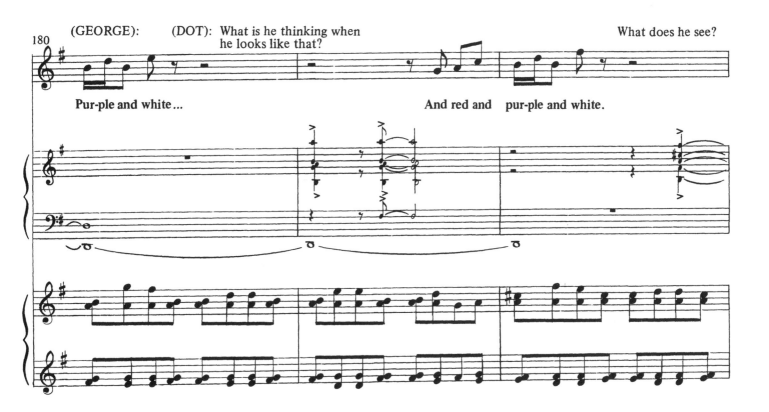

183 (DOT): Sometimes, not even blinking. *(To the young girls in the painting)*

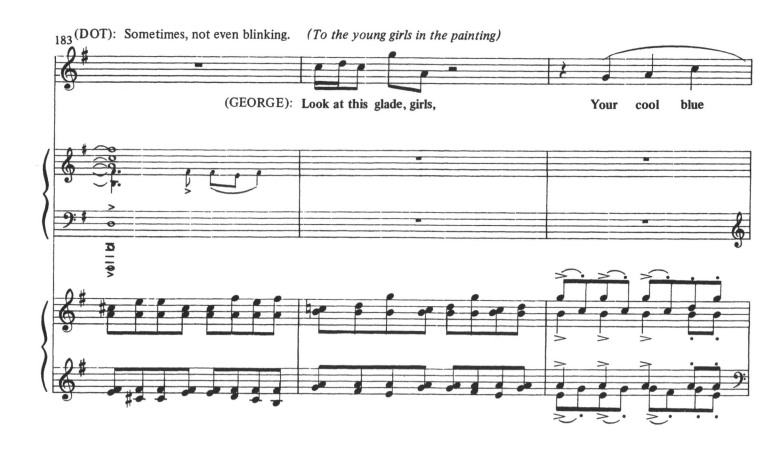

(GEORGE): Look at this glade, girls, Your cool blue

spot. No, stay in the shade, girls.

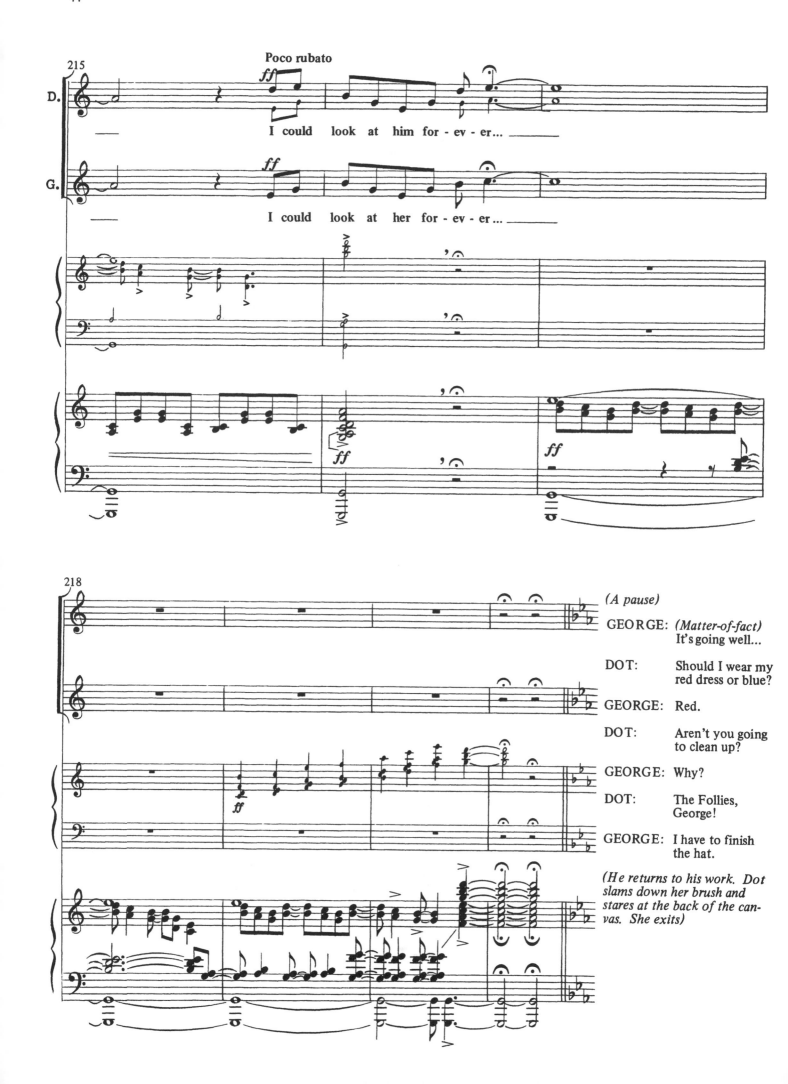

GEORGE: *(Matter-of-fact)* It's going well...

DOT: Should I wear my red dress or blue?

GEORGE: Red.

DOT: Aren't you going to clean up?

GEORGE: Why?

DOT: The Follies, George!

GEORGE: I have to finish the hat.

(He returns to his work. Dot slams down her brush and stares at the back of the canvas. She exits)

No. 8C   COLOR AND LIGHT (Part IV)
                             (GEORGE)

(Lights fade Downstage)

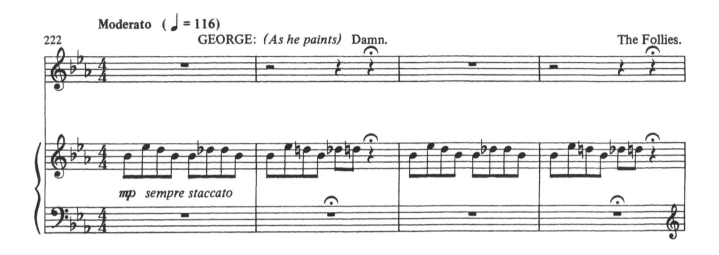

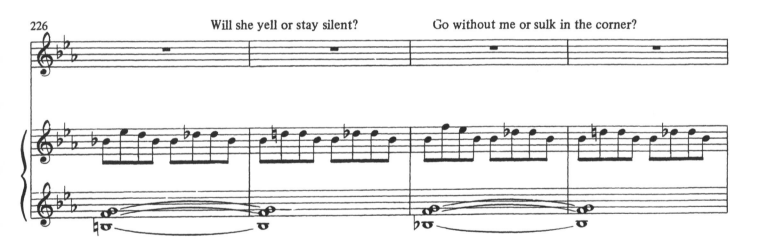

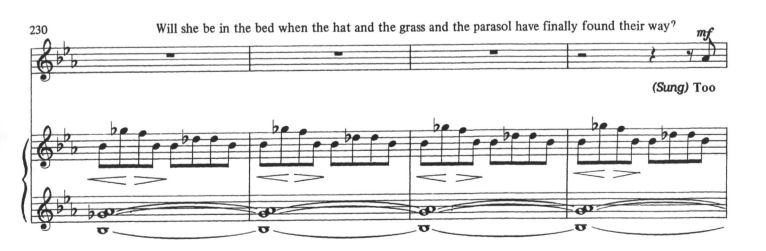

(He is consumed by light)

No. 9

SCENE CHANGE TO PARK

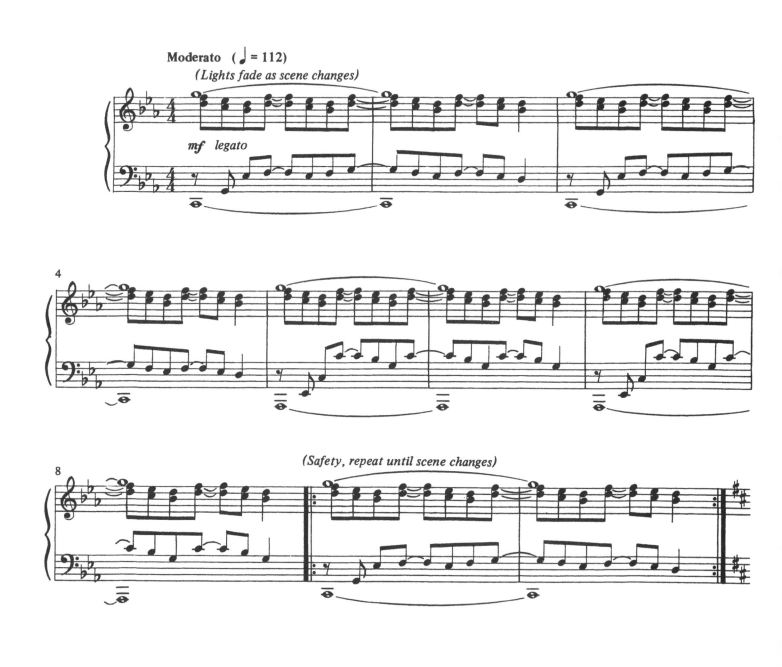

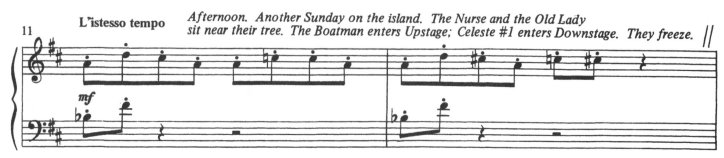

*Celeste #2 enters, as does George, who raises a cutout of
the Boatman's dog (Spot) from the stage. All except George freeze.*

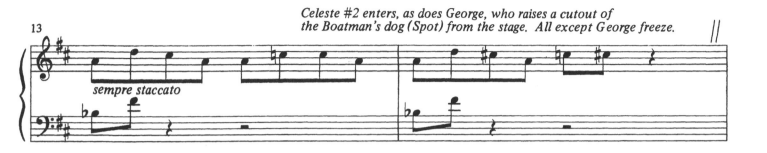

The Boatman pets his dog. The Celestes prepare to sit on a bench. All except George freeze.

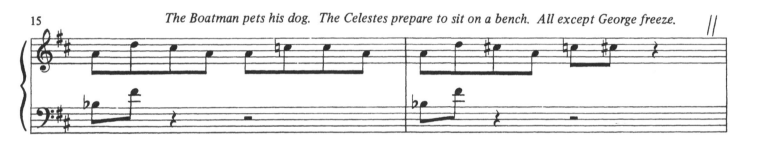

George starts to sketch the Boatman.   *The Celestes sit on a bench Stage Left.*

No. 10

GOSSIP SEQUENCE
(BOATMAN, CELESTE #1, CELESTE #2, NURSE, OLD LADY, JULES, YVONNE, GEORGE)

(Dot and Louis enter arm in arm. They look out at the water)

BOATMAN: I wear what I always wear -- then, I don't have to worry.

GEORGE: Worry?

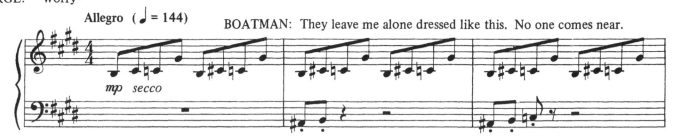

CELESTE #1: Look who's over there.   CELESTE #2: Dot. Who is she with?   CELESTE #1: Looks like

Louis the baker.   CELESTE #2: Well, how did Dot get to be with Louis?   CELESTE #1. She knows how to make dough rise!

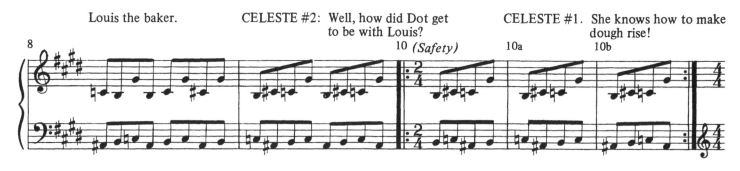

NURSE: *(Noticing Dot)* There is that woman.   OLD LADY: Who is she with?   NURSE: *(Squinting)* Looks like the baker.

OLD LADY: Moving up, I suppose.   NURSE: The artist is more handsome.   OLD LADY: You can not eat paintings,
my dear -- not when
there's bread in the oven.
(Safety)

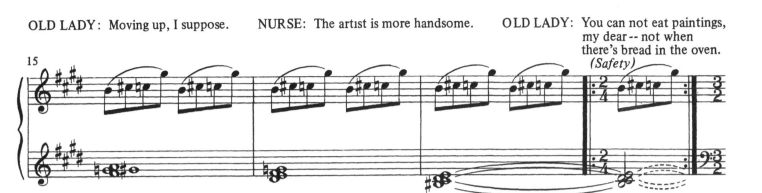

(Jules and Yvonne appear. They stand to one side and strike a pose)

Maestoso (♩ = 72)   JULES: They say he is working on an enormous canvas.

YVONNE: I heard somewhere   JULES: You heard it from me!   YVONNE: Look at him. Drawing a
he's painting little specks.   A large canvas of specks.
Really ...

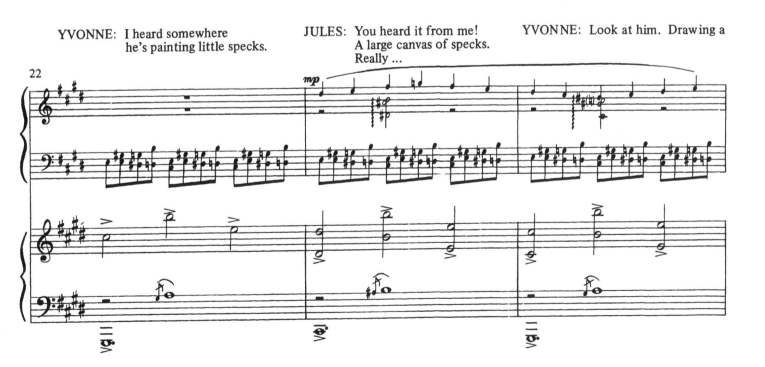

56

No. 11 CUES IN THE PARK

(Louise has come up to pet the dog. Boatman turns on her in a fury)

BOATMAN: Get away from that dog!

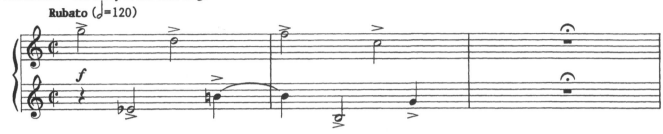

CELESTE #2: ... That's why he did not ask!   LOUIS: Creampuffs!

Segue

No. 12   THE DAY OFF (Part I)
(GEORGE, SPOT, FIFI)

(George, who has been staring at his sketch of Spot, looks over and sees that Dot and Louis have left)

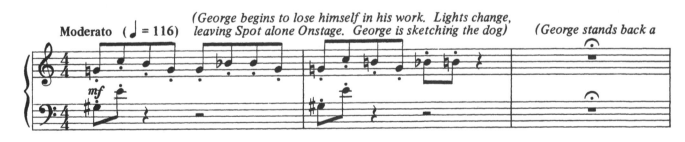

58

S.

58

Nose to the ground on Sun-day, *(Sniff, sniff)*

61

Stud-y-ing all the shoes and socks,___ Ev'ry-thing's worth it Sun-day,___

64

The day off. *(Sniff)* Bits of pas-try...

68

(Sniff) Piece of chick-en... *(Sniff)* Here's a hand-ker-chief That some-bod-y was sick in...

* Whenever "Fifi" sings.

* The Optional Ending is to be used if applause is desired following measure 121.
If the Optional Ending is used do not play bracketed measures 119 and 120.

No. 12A

THE DAY OFF (Part II)
(GEORGE, COMPANY)

The Horn Player rises from the Stage.

68

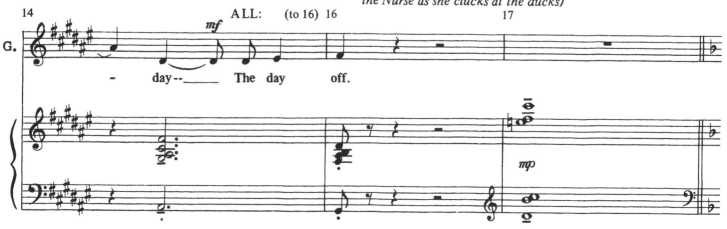

(George flips open a page of his sketchbook and starts to sketch the Nurse as she clucks at the ducks)

No. 12B   **THE DAY OFF (Part III)**
(GEORGE, NURSE)

Segue

No. 12C   THE DAY OFF (Part IV)

No. 12D

THE DAY OFF (Part V)
(GEORGE, FRANZ, FRIEDA)

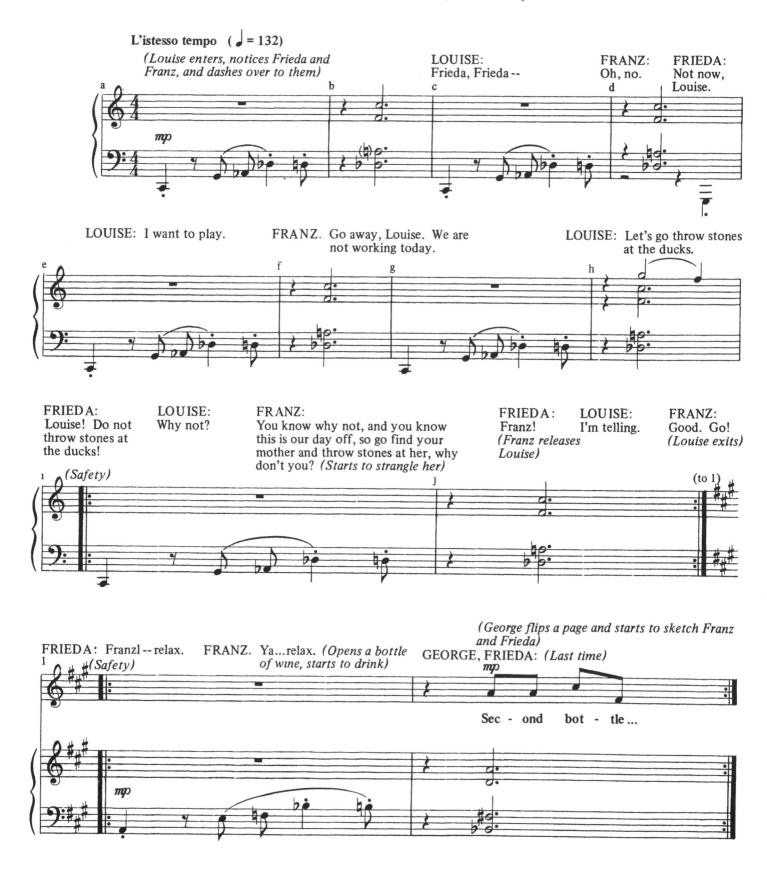

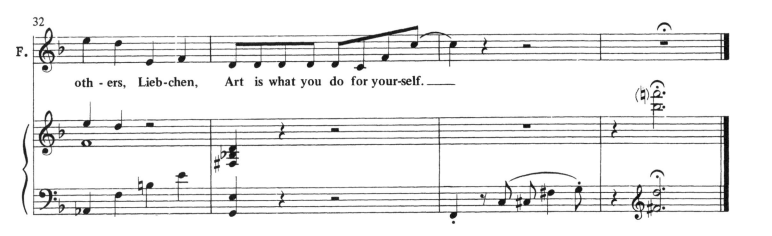

oth - ers, Lieb-chen, Art is what you do for your-self. ____

No. 12E THE DAY OFF (Part VI)
(GEORGE, BOATMAN)

GEORGE: *(Calling after Jules)* Jules. I would like you to come
to the studio sometime. See the new work ...

JULES.   For my approval?

GEORGE.   No, for your opinion.

JULES.   Very well.

(George flips a page over and starts sketching the Boatman)

You and me, pal,

We're the loon- ies.   Did you know that?   Bet you did -n't know that.

BOATMAN:

(to 11)

'Cause we tell them the truth!

Who you draw-ing? Who the hell you think you're draw-ing? Me? You don't know me!

Go on draw-ing. Since you're draw-ing on-ly what you want to see, an-y-way!

(Points to his patch)

One eye, no il-lu-sion-- That you get with two: _____

Segue

No. 12F

THE DAY OFF (Part VII)
(COMPANY)

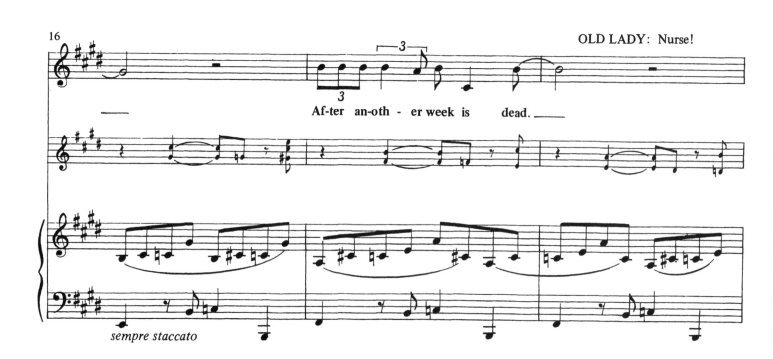

No. 13   EVERYBODY LOVES LOUIS
(DOT)

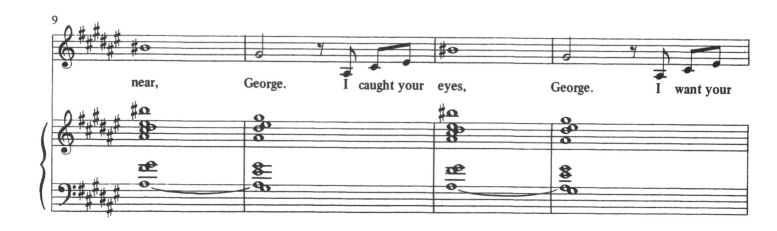

83

84

88

Lou-is it is!

No. 14   THE ONE ON THE LEFT
(GEORGE, CELESTE #1, CELESTE #2, SOLDIER)

Mr. and Mrs. exit.

Presto (♩. = 88)

(Vamp)

CELESTE #1: You really should try using that pole.
CELESTE #2: It will not make any difference.

CELESTE #1: Oh!   Oh!

CELESTE #2: What is wrong?   CELESTE #1: Just sit there.

(Celeste #1 carries on some more ["something huge!"] looking in the direction of the two soldiers. Soldiers converse for a moment, then come over)

(Vamp)

(George flips a page over)
(♩ = 112)
GEORGE, SOLDIER.

(Rumble from the Companion: Soldier raises hand to quiet him)

Ma- de - mois-elles, I and my friend, We are but sol - diers!

SOLDIER:

Pass - ing the time In be - tween wars For weeks at an end.

CELESTE #1 *(Aside)*   CELESTE #2:·   CELESTE #1

Both of them are per - fect. You can have the oth - er. I don't want the oth - er.

Segue subito

No. 15

FINISHING THE HAT
(GEORGE)

(George is alone. He moves Downstage, near
Fifi the pug who rises, and sits)

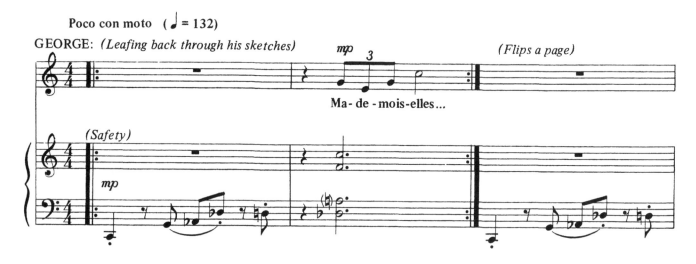

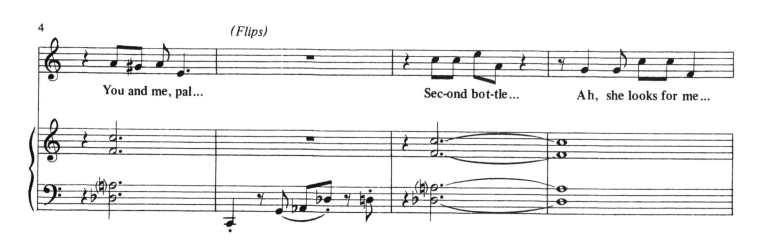

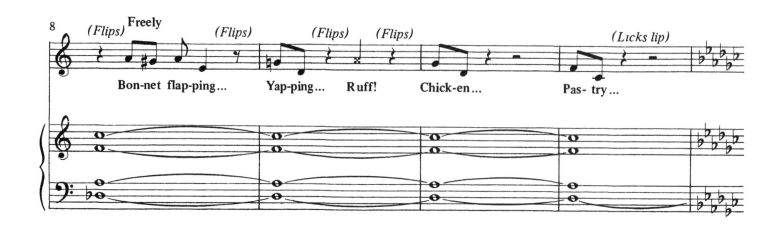

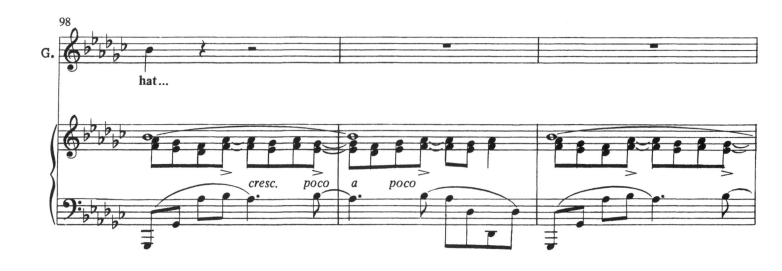

hat...

Where there nev-er was a   hat ...

No. 16   BUSTLE

Note: At measure 3, cast enters one at a time, each singing an excerpt from songs sung earlier in the show, out of rhythm and in any key, gradually getting louder and faster.

Cue: MR. *(Spotting Louis, who has entered in search of Dot)*
     Isn't that the baker?

     MRS. **Why, yes it is!** *(They cross to Louis. George brings on the Hornplayer cut-out. Old Lady enters)*

OLD LADY:
Where is
that tree?
Nurse! Nurse!

(Dot enters, and suddenly she and George are still, staring

Slow (♩ = 88)

Maestoso

at one another. Everyone Onstage turns slowly to them. People begin to sing fragments of songs. Dot and George move

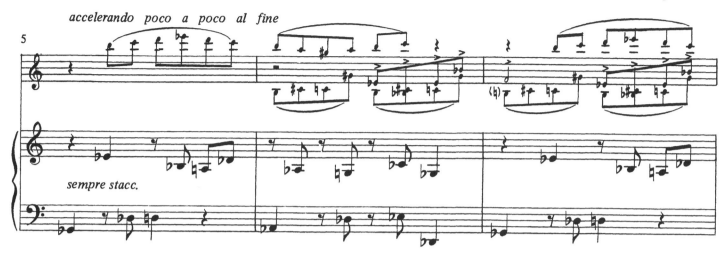

closer to one another, circling each other like gun duellers. The rest of the cast close in around them until Dot and George

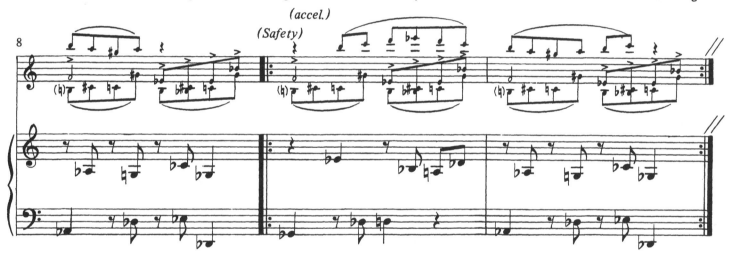

stop, opposite each other. Silence. Dot takes her bustle and defiantly turns it around, creating a pregnant stance. There is an audible gasp from the onlookers. Lights fade to black)

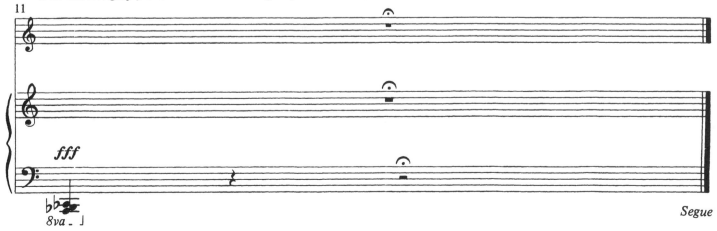

Segue

No. 17

SCENE CHANGE TO STUDIO

No. 18

WE DO NOT BELONG TOGETHER
(DOT, GEORGE)

GEORGE: *(Getting angry)* ...Why are you telling me this? First, you
ask for a painting that is *not* yours -- then you tell me this. *(Beginning
to return to studio)* I have work to do.

Freely (♩ = 112)

DOT: Yes, George, run to your work. Hide behind your painting.   I have come to tell you I am leaving

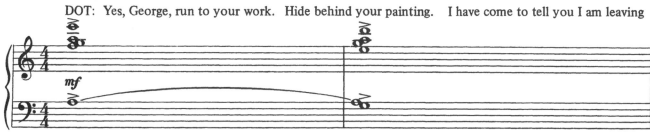

because I thought you might *care* to know -- foolish of
me, because you care about nothing.

GEORGE: I care about many things --
DOT: Things -- not people.
GEORGE: People, too.

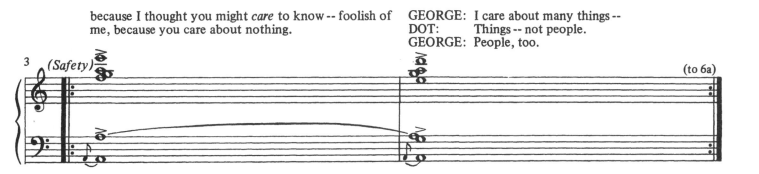

GEORGE: *(cont'd)* I cannot divide my feelings as neatly as you and, I am not
hiding behind my canvas -- I am living in it.

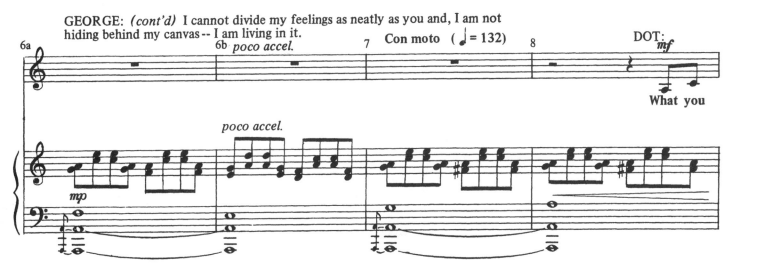

What you

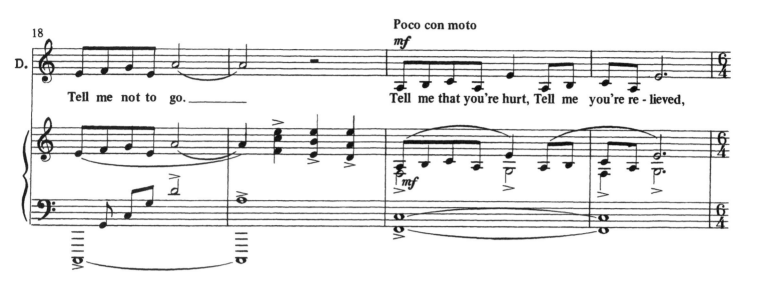

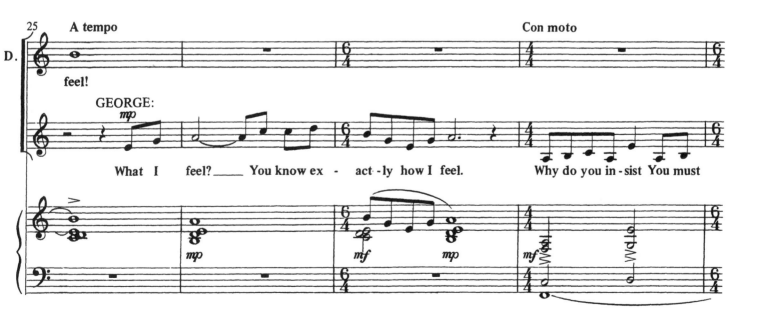

hear the words, When you know I can-not give you words? Not the ones you

need. _____ There's

noth-ing to say.___ I can-not be what___ you want.___

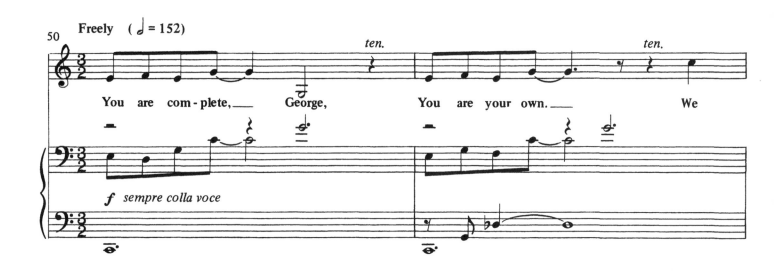

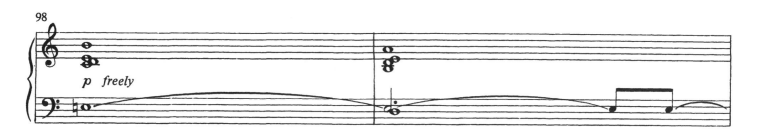

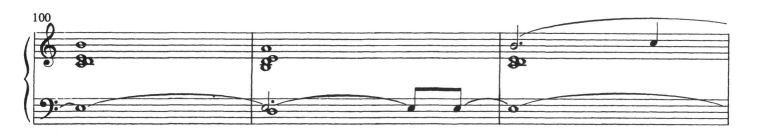

The set changes back to the park scene around him. When the change is complete, he moves Downstage Right with the Old Lady, and begins to draw her. They are alone Onstage, except for the cut-out of the Soldier's Companion, which stands towards the rear of the stage. There is a change of tone in both George and the Old Lady. She has assumed a kind of loving attitude, soft and dream-like. George is rather sullen in her presence.)

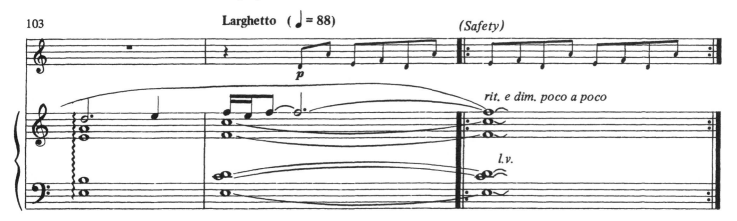

No. 19

BEAUTIFUL
(OLD LADY, GEORGE)

OLD LADY: And now, look across there --

Andante (𝅗𝅥 = 66)   Poco con moto (𝅗𝅥 = 72)

OLD LADY: *(cont'd)* -- in the distance -- all those beautiful trees cut down for a foolish tower.

How I loved the view from here ...   OLD LADY:

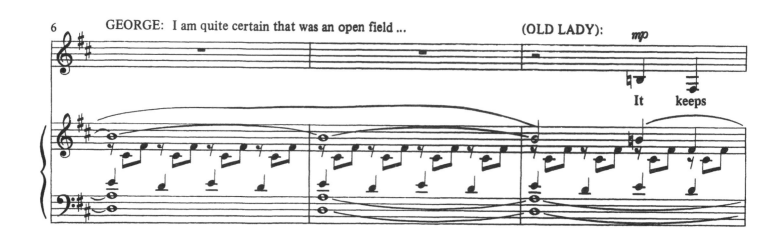

GEORGE: I am quite certain that was an open field ...   (OLD LADY):

121

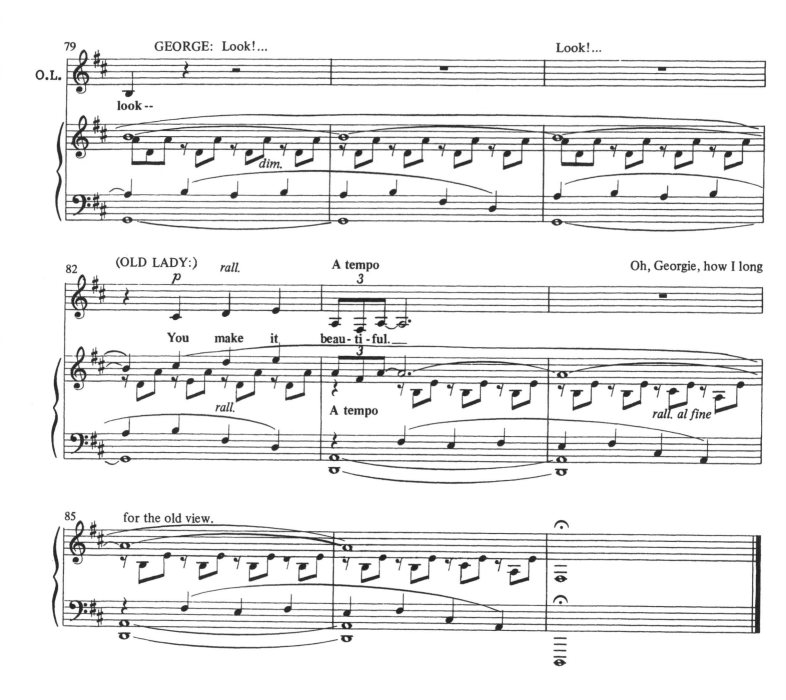

No. 20   SOLDIER CUE #1

SOLDIER: She did seem rather pushy.

CELESTE #2: Very! And he was so odd.

SOLDIER: *(Annoyed)* He is not odd.

CELESTE #2: No. No, I didn't
              really mean odd...

No. 21   JULES AND FRIEDA

GEORGE: Connect, George ... Connect ...

(Fade upon repeat)

No. 22   SOLDIER CUES #2 and #3

CELESTE #2: I do not care if she never speaks to me again.

SOLDIER: She won't.

SOLDIER. Let's go say hello to Celeste.

CELESTE #2: *(Indignant)* I do not wish to speak with her!

SOLDIER: Come. It will be fun!

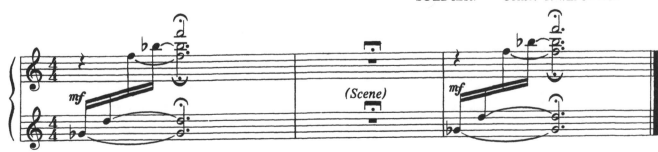

126

No. 23   CHAOS

YVONNE: Your father is in the studio.

LOUISE: No, he's not. He's with Frieda. I saw them.

FRANZ: Where?

LOUISE: Over there. Tonguing.

* *Each melodic cell enters where indicated. Ad lib. any fast tempo (do not coordinate with ♩ = 186) repeating the figures until the cut-off. Chaotic cacophony will be the desired result. For rehearsal purposes, the pianist should freely alternate the figures while depressing the sustain pedal.*

No. 24   SUNDAY
(COMPANY)

(George and the Old Lady have been watching the chaos. Arpeggiated chord, as at the beginning of the play. Everybody suddenly freezes in place)

OLD LADY: Remember, George.
(She turns back to the water)

GEORGE: *(Turns to the group, mutters)* Order. *(Everyone turns simultaneously to George)*

(As chords continue under, George looks at each of the people one by one and we see his ultimate power over his subjects. He nods to them, and each ends up in one of the posed positions that they held at some point earlier in the act.)

(GEORGE): Design. *(George nods to Frieda and Franz and they cross Downstage Right onto the apron)*

(George nods to Mr. and Mrs. and they cross Upstage) Tension. *(George nods to Celestes #1 and #2 and they cross Downstage)* *(Jules and Yvonne cross Upstage Right)*

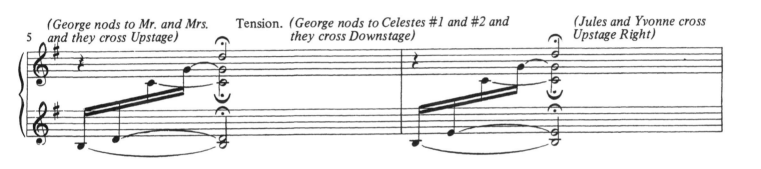

Balance. *(Old Lady crosses Right as Dot crosses Center)* *(Soldier crosses Upstage Right)* (to 17)

(George gestures to the Boatman, who crosses Downstage Right)

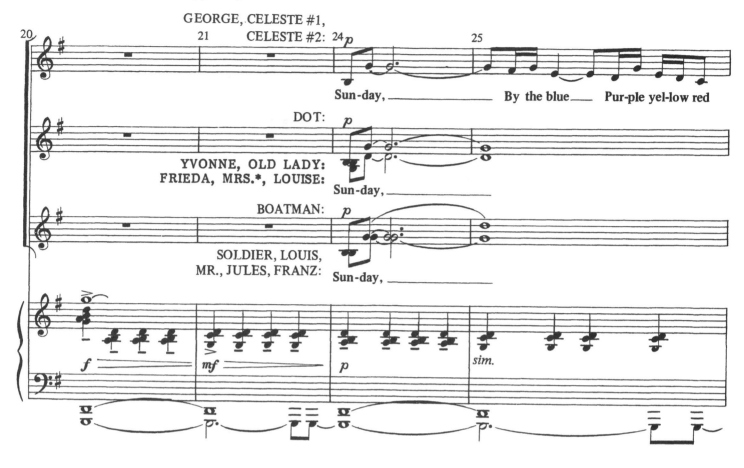

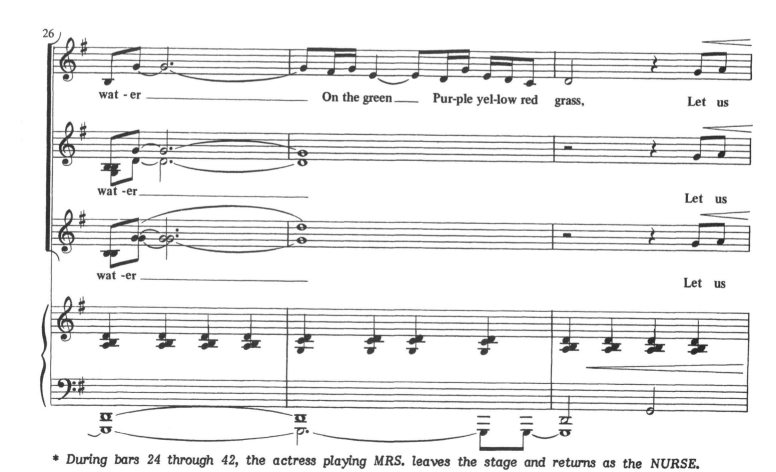

* *During bars 24 through 42, the actress playing MRS. leaves the stage and returns as the NURSE.*

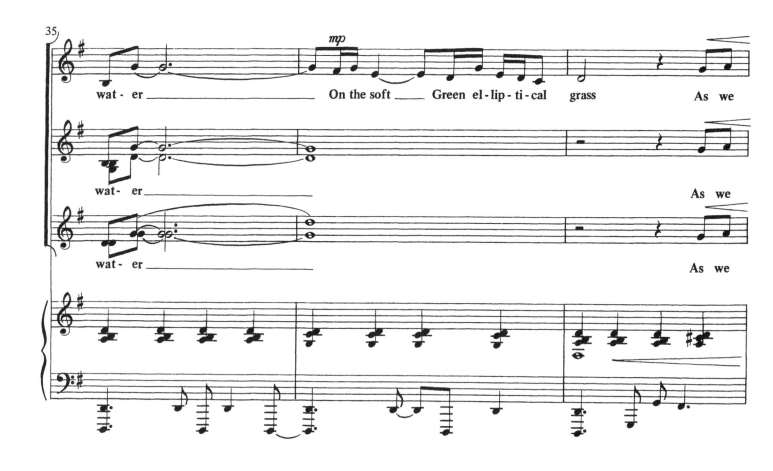

35

wat - er _____ On the soft _____ Green el - lip - ti - cal grass As we

wat - er _____ As we

wat - er _____ As we

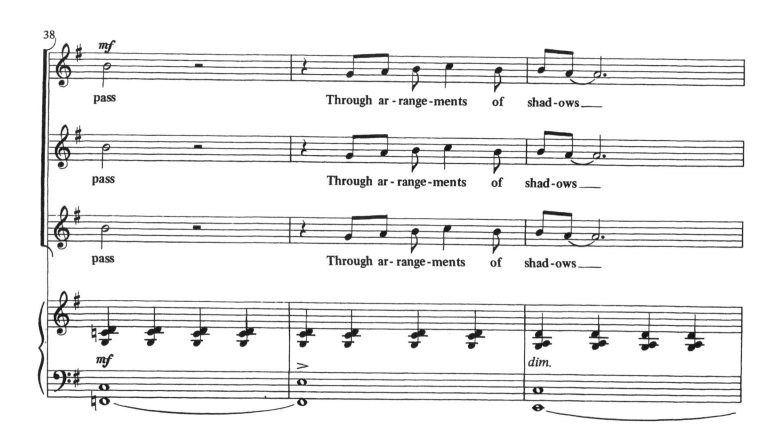

38

mf

pass Through ar - range - ments of shad - ows ___

pass Through ar - range - ments of shad - ows ___

pass Through ar - range - ments of shad - ows ___

mf   *dim.*

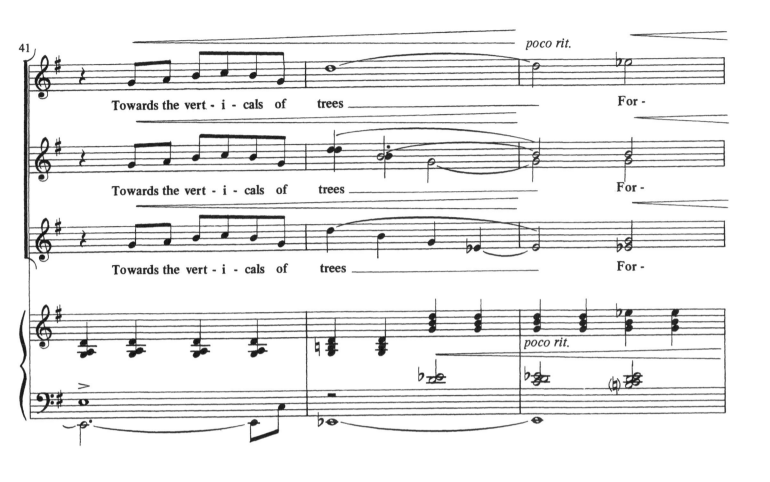

On the green ____ Or-ange vi - o - let mass   Of the grass

Of the grass

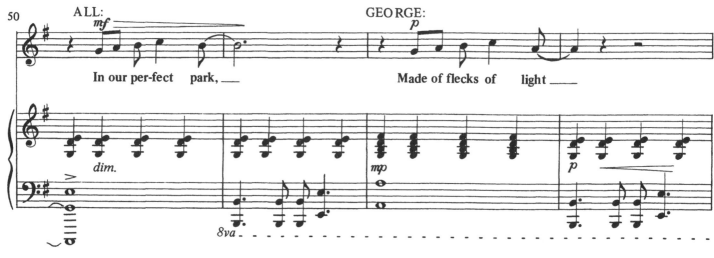

In our per-fect park, ___   Made of flecks of light ___

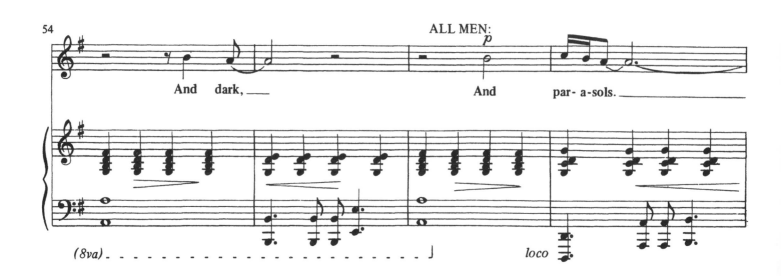

And dark, ___   And par- a-sols. _____

End of Act I

ACT II

No. 25

IT'S HOT UP HERE
(COMPANY)

(Lights slowly fade up, and we see Everyone frozen in the tableau. There is a very long pause before we begin. The audience should feel the tension as they wait for something to happen. Finally, Music begins.)

137

SOLDIER: I like the one in the light hat. *(Safety)*

DOT: *(Last time only)* *p cantabile*

144

ALL

out-ward show   Of bliss up here   Is   dis-ap-pear-ing dot by   dot.

dim. poco

And it's

a   poco

p

f

f

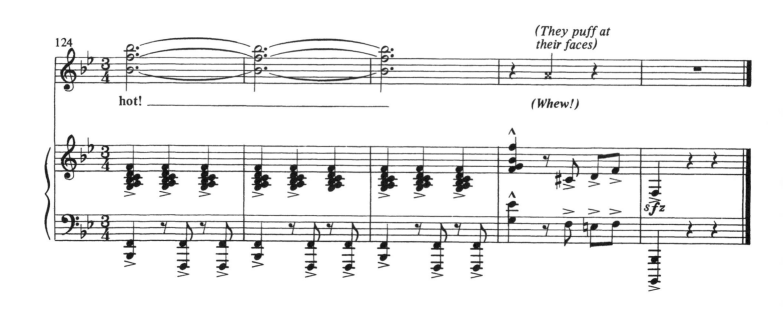

(They puff at their faces)

hot! _____

(Whew!)

sfz

No. 26   EULOGIES

*In the following section, the characters break from their poses when they speak,
and they exit when they finish. Accompanying each exit, a piece of scenery flies
out, so that by the time the Boatman exits at the end of the sequence, the set will
be returned to its original white configuration.*

(Immediately after the applause)

Unmeasured

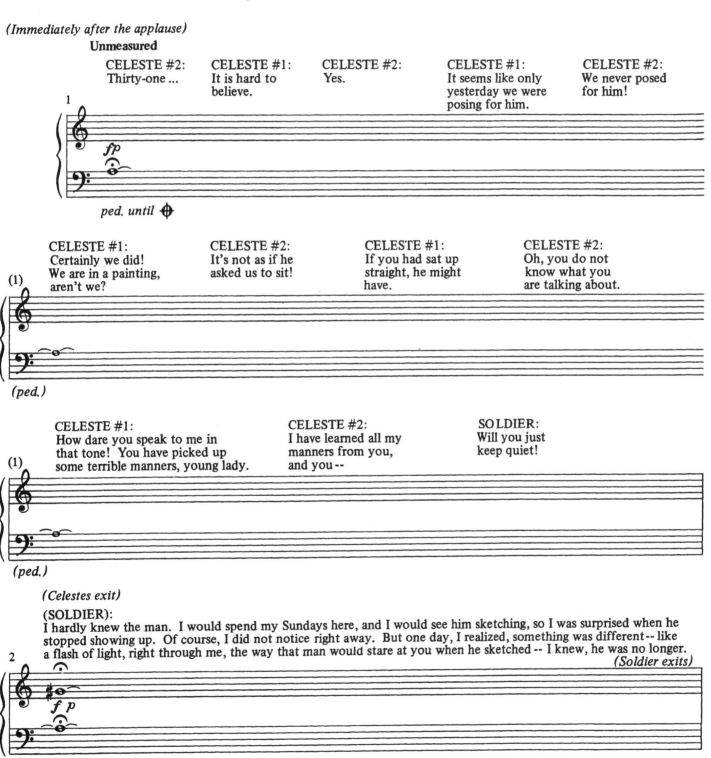

CELESTE #2:
Thirty-one ...

CELESTE #1:
It is hard to
believe.

CELESTE #2:
Yes.

CELESTE #1:
It seems like only
yesterday we were
posing for him.

CELESTE #2:
We never posed
for him!

ped. until ⊕

CELESTE #1:
Certainly we did!
We are in a painting,
aren't we?

CELESTE #2:
It's not as if he
asked us to sit!

CELESTE #1:
If you had sat up
straight, he might
have.

CELESTE #2:
Oh, you do not
know what you
are talking about.

(ped.)

CELESTE #1:
How dare you speak to me in
that tone! You have picked up
some terrible manners, young lady.

CELESTE #2:
I have learned all my
manners from you,
and you --

SOLDIER:
Will you just
keep quiet!

(ped.)

(Celestes exit)

(SOLDIER):
I hardly knew the man. I would spend my Sundays here, and I would see him sketching, so I was surprised when he
stopped showing up. Of course, I did not notice right away. But one day, I realized, something was different-- like
a flash of light, right through me, the way that man would stare at you when he sketched -- I knew, he was no longer.

(Soldier exits)

f p

(ped.)

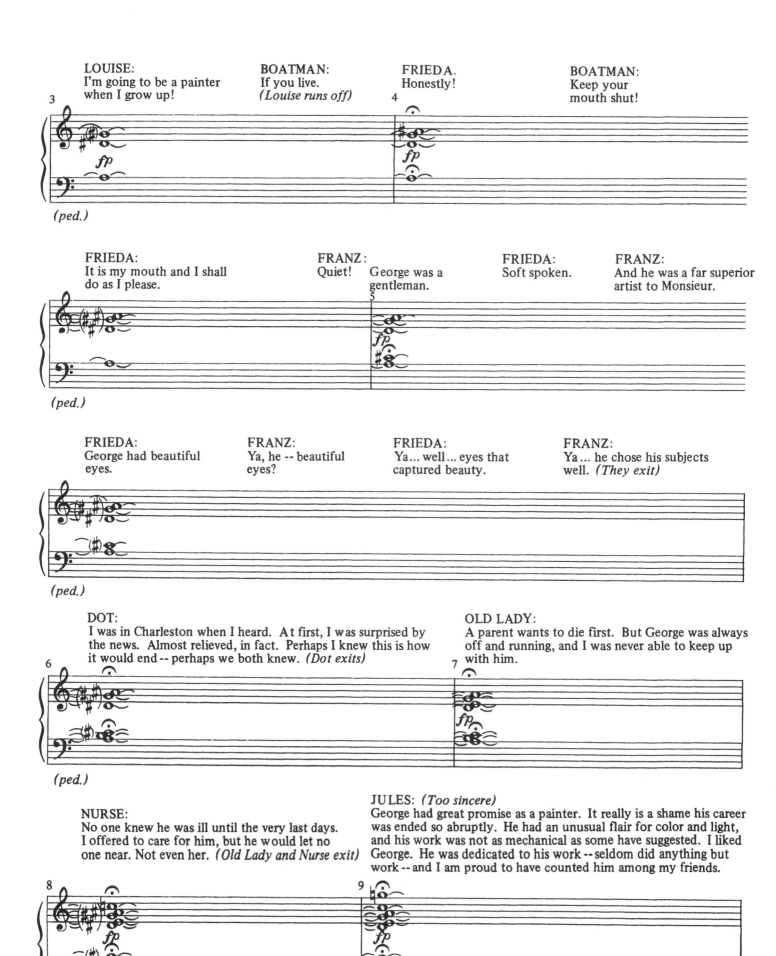

YVONNE:
George stopped me once in the park -- it was the only time I had ever spoken to him outside the company of Jules. He stared at my jacket for an instant, then muttered something about beautiful colors and just walked on. I father fancied George. *(Jules looks at her)* Well, most of the women did. *(Jules and Yvonne exit)*

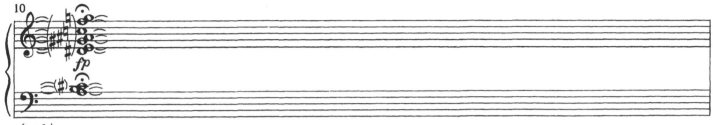

(ped.)

BOATMAN:
They all wanted him and hated him at the same time. They wanted to be painted -- splashed on some fancy salon wall. But they hated him, too. Hated him because he only spoke when he absolutely had to. Most of all they hated him be - cause they knew he would always be around. *(Boatman exits)*

(ped.)

The stage is bare. Lights change. It is 1984. We are in the auditorium of the museum where the painting now hangs. Enter George. He wheels in his grandmother, Marie (played by Dot), who is ninety-eight and confined to a wheelchair. Dennis, George's technical assistant, rolls on a control console. An immense white machine rolls on. Our contemporary George is an inventor-sculptor and this is his latest invention, the Chromolume #7. The machine is post-modern in design and is dom-

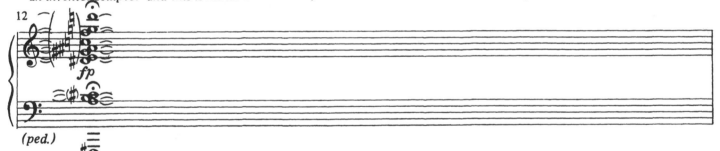

(ped.)

inated by a four-foot-in-diameter sphere at the top. It glows with a range of cool colored light. Marie sits on one side of the machine, and George is at the console on the other side. Behind them is a full-stage projection screen.

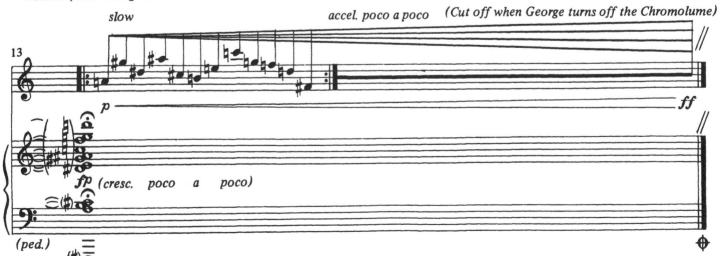

(ped.)

No. 27   CHROMOLUME #7 (Part I)

GEORGE: On this occasion, I present my latest Chromolume --

MARIE: -- Number Seven --

GEORGE: -- which pays homage to "La Grande Jatte" and to my grandmother, Marie. The score for this presentation has been composed by Naomi Eisen.

Naomi enters, bows, exits.

Freely, sustained

Strobe lights begin emitting from the Chromolume

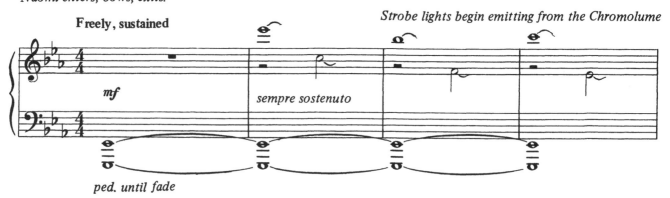

along with side shafts of brilliant light. Colors begin to fill the stage and audience, creating a pointillistic look. Just as the

sphere begins to illuminate, producing various images from the painting, there is a sudden explosion of sparks and smoke. (Imitate power breakdown by playing descending chromatic clusters and fading out.) The lighting system flickers on and off until everything dies, including the music. There is a moment of chaos in the darkness.

(Repeat as needed)

No. 28

CHROMOLUME #7 (Part II)

In the New York production, much of the music for Chromolume #7 *was pre-programmed on several synthesizers and sequencers. These instruments and equipment were interfaced using MIDI (Musical Instrument Digital Interface).*

The piece is constructed of motivic cells that are cued and repeated as indicated in the score. Each of the nine Cues begins after the dialog cue or after the specified amount of time (in seconds).

Because the instruments and equipment available in subsequent productions will most likely be different than those used in the New York production, the programming of the musical components, using these motivic cells, for each production will be the responsibility of the Musical Director.

GEORGE: We're definitely ready, Bob.

GREENBERG: Well ... proceed. Proceed!

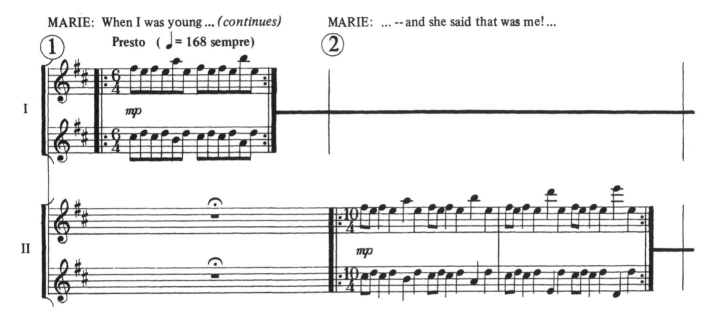

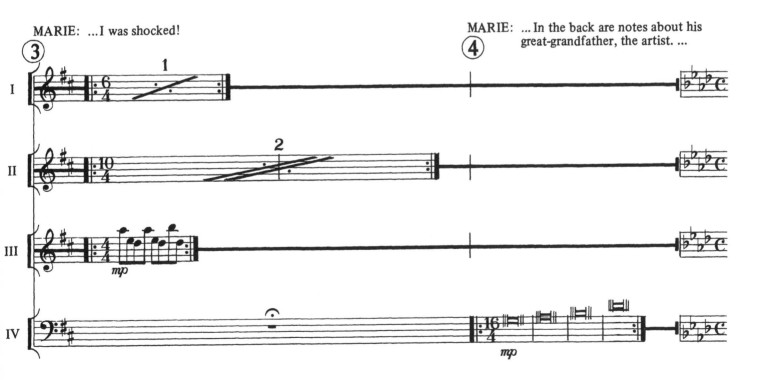

152

GEORGE: ...It will be on
exhibition here in
the upstairs gallery
until August first.

(Center laser is activated)

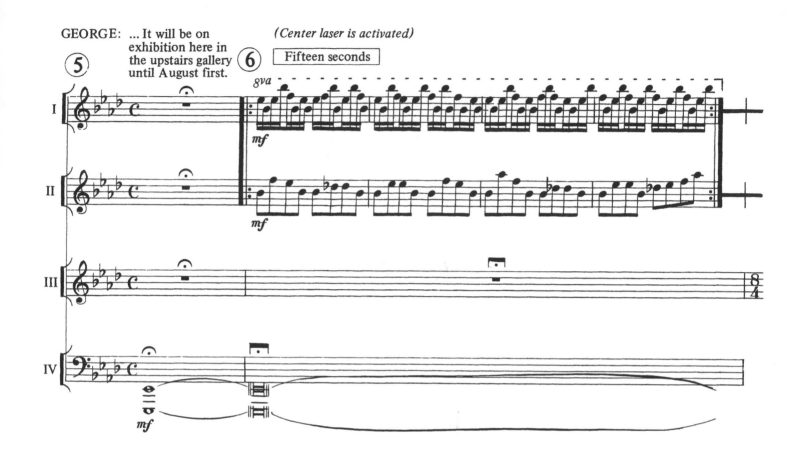

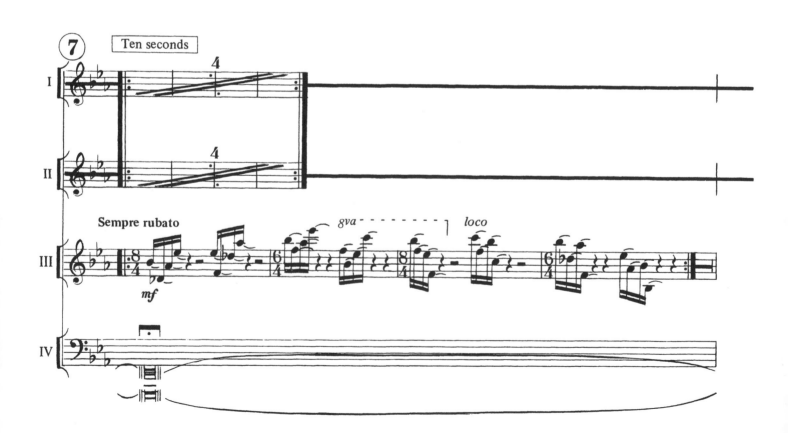

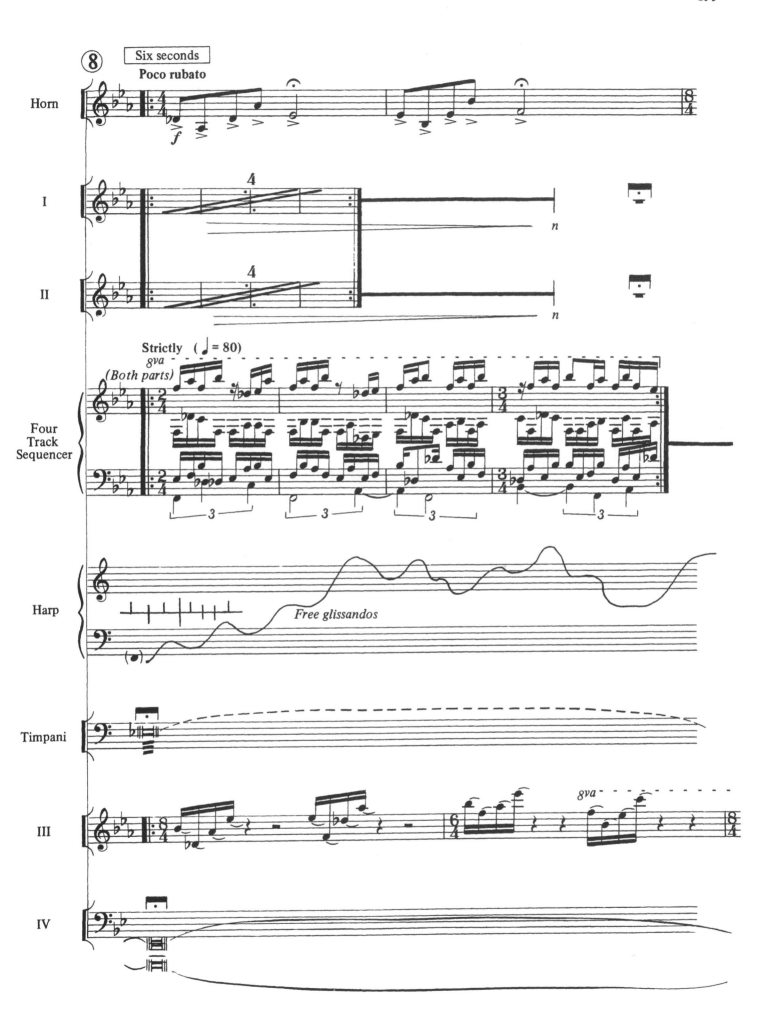

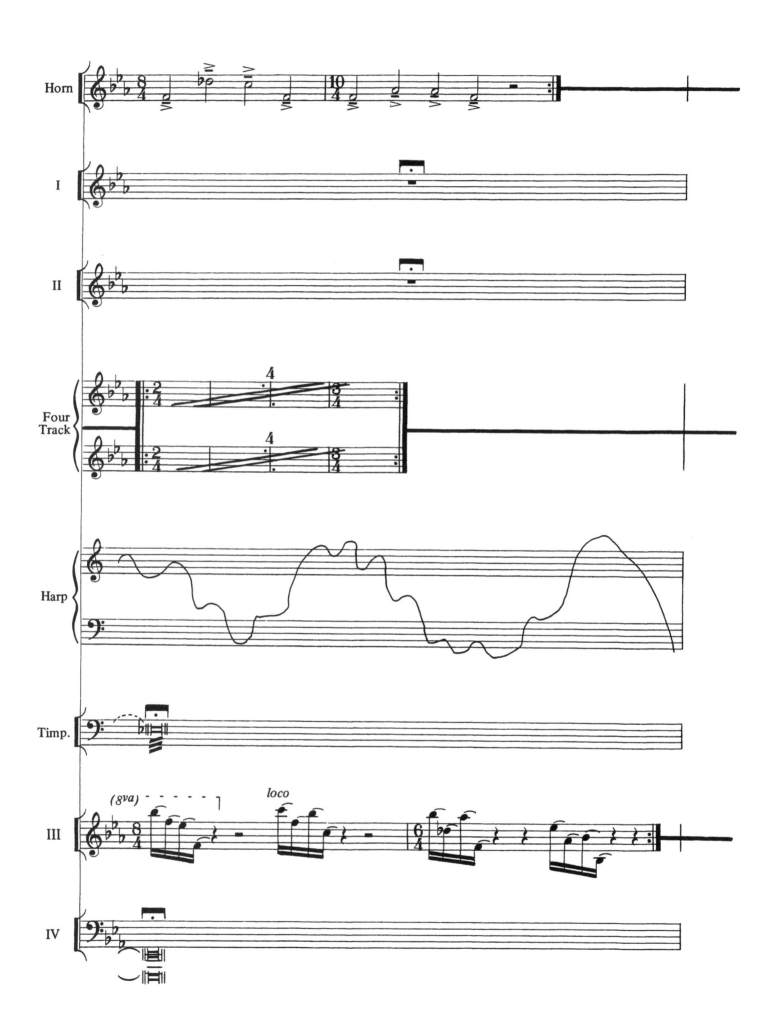

155

156

Begin fade as painting descends, covering the Chro-molume

Segue subito

No. 29

PUTTING IT TOGETHER (Part I)
(COCKTAIL MUSIC #1)

(We are now in the gallery where the painting hangs and in front
of which the reception is beginning. Harriet and Billy enter,
closely followed by Redmond, Greenberg, Alex, Betty, and Naomi.)

Segue

No. 29A

PUTTING IT TOGETHER (Part II)
(HARRIET, BILLY)

NAOMI: I thought it went very well, except for that electrical foul-up.
What did you guys think?

ALEX: Terrible. **BETTY:** *(Simultaneously)* Terrific.

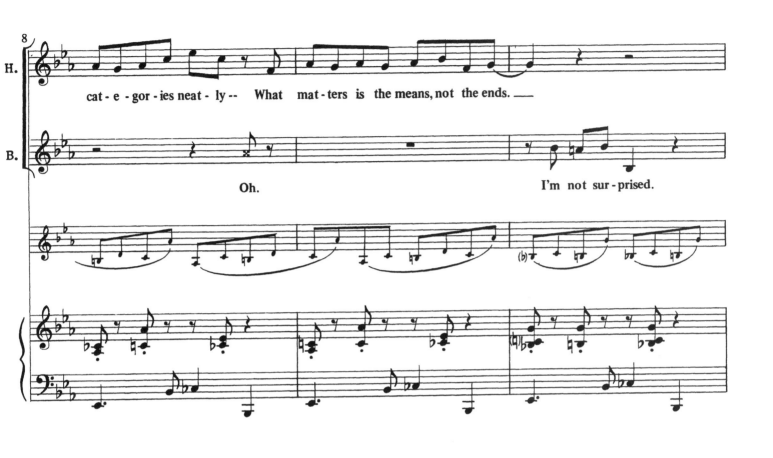

cat - e - gor - ies neat - ly -- What mat - ters is the means, not the ends. ___

Oh.   I'm not sur - prised.

That is the state ___ of the art, ___ my dear,   That is the state of the

That is the state ___ of the art, ___ my dear,   That is the state of the

Segue

No. 29B

PUTTING IT TOGETHER (Part III)
(GREENBERG, REDMOND)

yes-ter-day's for-got-ten.   There's no sur-prise.

(Nods)

And to - mor-row is al-read-y pas-sé. _____

That is the state ___ of the art, ___ my friend,   That is the state of the

That is the state ___ of the art, ___ my friend,   That is the state of the

Segue

162

No. 29C   **PUTTING IT TOGETHER (Part IV)**
(NAOMI, BETTY, ALEX)

Segue

No. 29D

PUTTING IT TOGETHER (Part V)
(COMPANY)

Segue

No. 29E

PUTTING IT TOGETHER (Part VI)
(GEORGE)

(George makes a grand entrance with Marie, who is in a wheelchair, and Elaine. Applause from guests. George and Marie move towards the painting. Lights come down on George)

Cross-fade segue

No. 29F   PUTTING IT TOGETHER (Part VII)
(COCKTAIL MUSIC #2)

No. 29G   **PUTTING IT TOGETHER (Part VIII)**
(GEORGE)

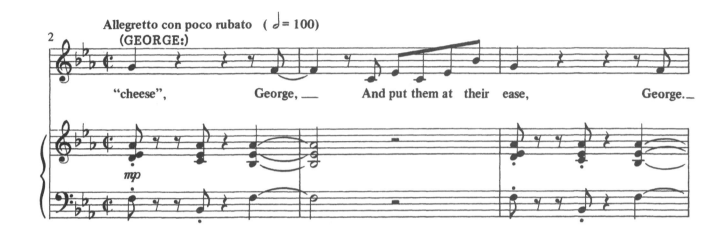

Cross-fade segue

No. 29H

PUTTING IT TOGETHER (Part IX)
(COCKTAIL MUSIC #3)

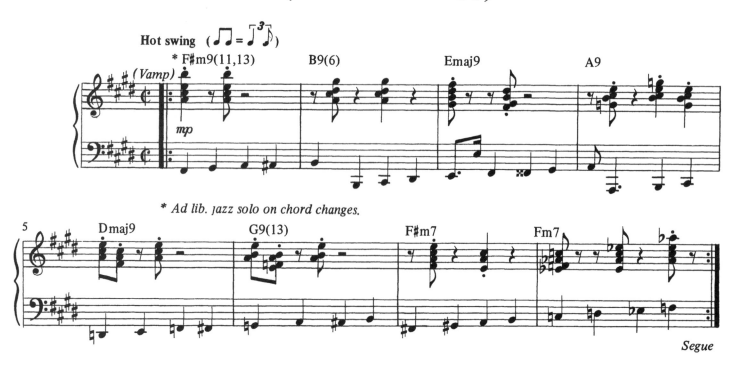

* *Ad lib. jazz solo on chord changes.*

Segue

No. 291

PUTTING IT TOGETHER (Part X)
(GEORGE)

MARIE:
...George and I are going back to France
next month to visit the island where the
painting was made, and George is going
to bring the Lomochrome.

GEORGE:
Chromolume. I've been invited by
the government to do a presentation
of the machine on the island.

MARIE:
George has never been to France.

GEORGE:
(To audience)

*(He raises a cutout
of himself in front
of Billy and Harriet)*

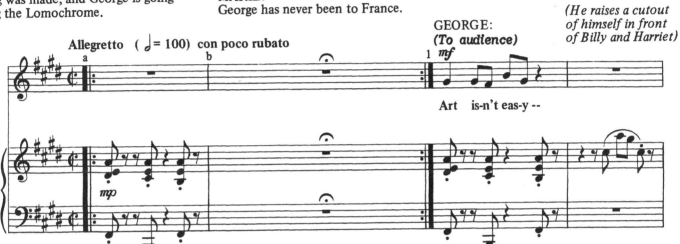

Art is-n't eas-y --

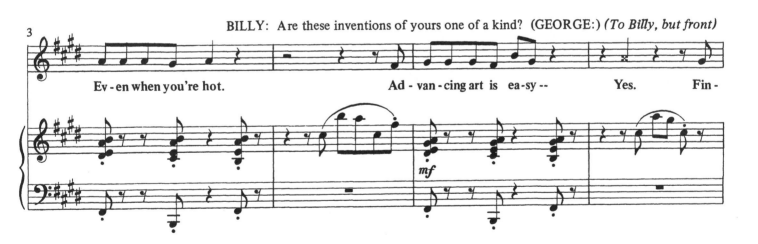

BILLY: Are these inventions of yours one of a kind? (GEORGE:) *(To Billy, but front)*

Ev - en when you're hot.   Ad - van - cing art is ea-sy --   Yes.   Fin -

MARIE:
They take a year to make.

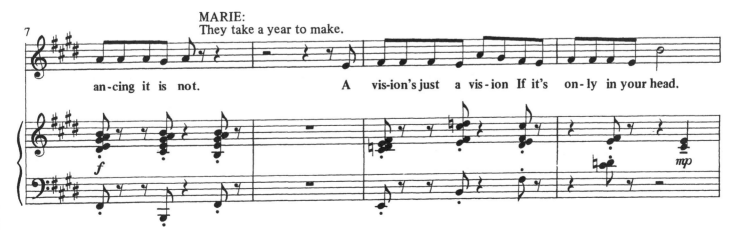

an - cing it is not.   A vis-ion's just a vis - ion If it's on - ly in your head.

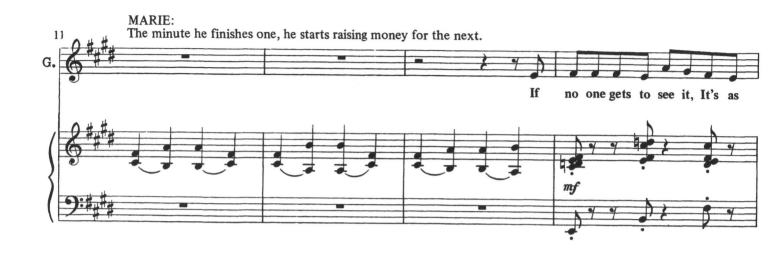

MARIE:
The minute he finishes one, he starts raising money for the next.

If no one gets to see it, It's as

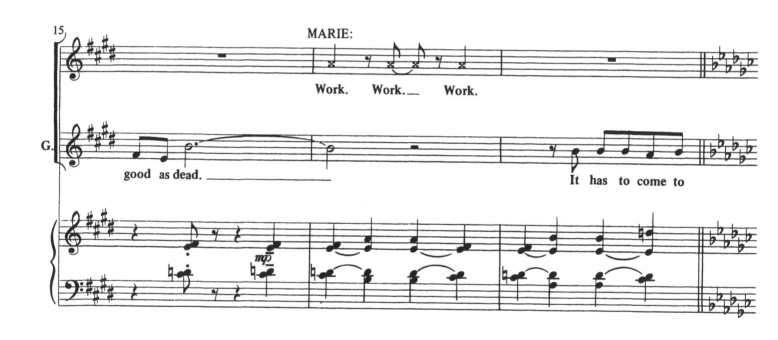

MARIE:

Work. Work.— Work.

good as dead._____

It has to come to

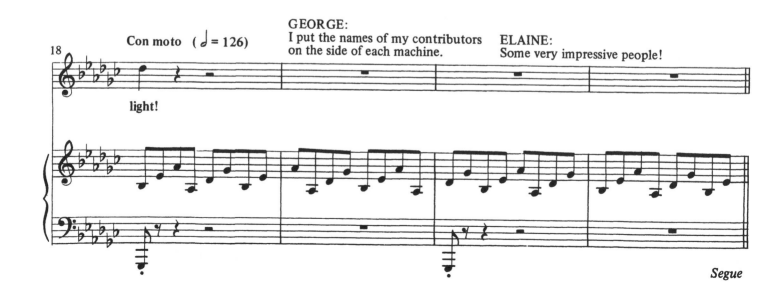

Con moto (♩ = 126)

GEORGE:
I put the names of my contributors
on the side of each machine.

ELAINE:
Some very impressive people!

light!

Segue

No. 29J

PUTTING IT TOGETHER (Part XI)
(GEORGE)

HARRIET:
Well, we must speak further. My family has a foundation
and we are always looking for new projects.

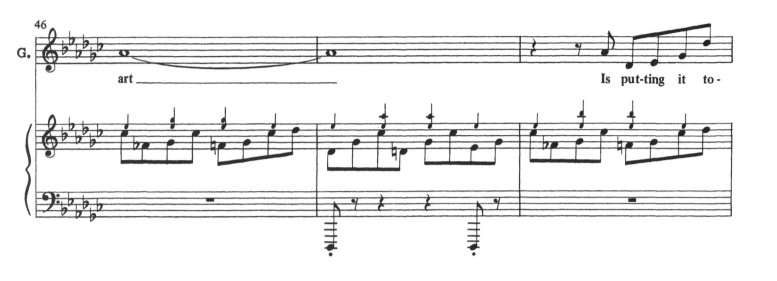

art _____ Is put-ting it to-

geth- er   Bit   by   bit ...

(Dialogue)   (Safety)

Segue

No. 29K

PUTTING IT TOGETHER (Part XII)
(GEORGE)

65

G.

sion And an ex-hi - bi - tion in ad-di - tion?_

Segue

No. 29L

PUTTING IT TOGETHER (Part XIII)
(COMPANY)

L'istesso tempo (♩ = 116)

ALL:

ALEX,
BETTY:

ALL:

Art is -n't ea - sy-- Try-ing to make con-nec - tions-- Who un-der-stands it --?

HARRIET,
BILLY:

ALL:

GREENBERG,
REDMOND:

Dif - fi-cult to e - val - u - ate-- Art is - n't ea - sy-- Try-ing to form col - lec - tions--

7 ALL: NAOMI: *(To whoever will listen)* ALL:

Al - ways in tran-sit -- And then when you have to col-lab-or - ate --! Art is - n't ea - sy, ____

10

____ An - y way you look at it ...

Cross-fade segue

No. 29M

PUTTING IT TOGETHER (Part XIV)
(COCKTAIL MUSIC #4)

Bossa nova *(repeat ad lib. under dialogue)*

(Vamp)

Segue

No. 29N   **PUTTING IT TOGETHER (Part XV)**
(GEORGE)

RANDOLPH:
There's a lot of opportunity for some
nice press here. *(George raises a third
cutout of himself)*

G.

___ sion, Which will cause a crack in the foun-da - tion. You'll have wast -ed

all that con - ver-sa - tion.

DENNIS:
I am really sorry, George...*(etc.)*...

Cocktail style, rubato

p legato

GEORGE: DENNIS:
What? I'm quitting...*(etc.)*...

Segue

No. 290   PUTTING IT TOGETHER (Part XVI)
(GEORGE)

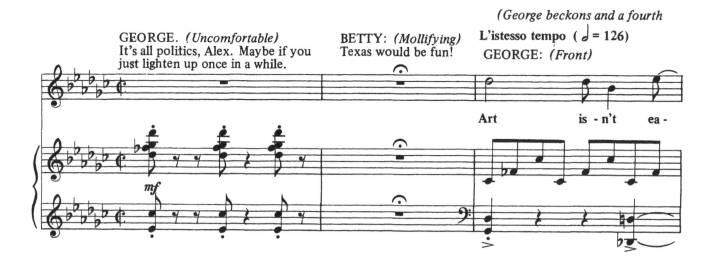

Attacca subito

No. 29P

PUTTING IT TOGETHER (Part XVII)
(GEORGE, COMPANY)

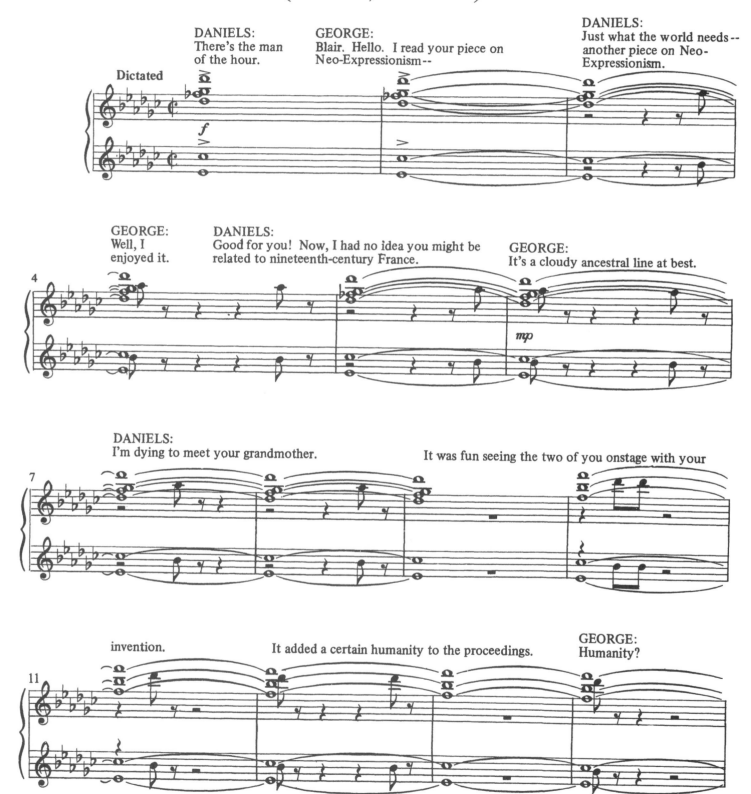

194

(As she turns briefly away from him and rummages through her purse
for a cigarette, George rushes offstage and brings on cut-out #5, which
he sets up in front of her during the following)

DANIELS:
Don't get me wrong. You're a talented guy. If you weren't, I wouldn't

Con moto (𝅘𝅥 = 116)

GEORGE:

I dis - a - gree.

waste our time with my opinion. I think you are capable of far more. Not that you couldn't succeed
by doing Chromolume after Chromolume -- but there are new discoveries to be made, George.

(Vamp)   (She holds up her cigarette and waits for a light from the cut-out)

GEORGE:
(Last time) *mf* (to 38)

Be

new,   George.   They tell you till they're blue,   George:

You're new or else you're through,   George,   And ev - en if it's

G.
_ tion -- Lin-ing up a

BETTY: *mp*
...He's an or - i - gin - al...

ALEX:
...Was...

(During the following, all the cut-outs falter sporadically, causing George to move more and more rapidly among them)

77
cresc. poco a poco

G.
prom - i - nent com-mis - sion And an ex -hi - bi - tion in add - i -

80

G.
_ tion, Here a lit - tle dab of pol - i - ti - cian, There a lit - tle

BETTY: *mp*
I like those im - a - ges.

198

No. 30

CHILDREN AND ART
(MARIE)

ELAINE:
... tonight was a wonderful experience for Marie. I don't remember seeing her so hap-py. It was very good of you to include her.

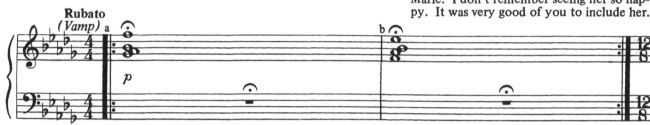

GEORGE:
She is something, isn't she?

ELAINE:
Yes, she is ...

MARIE:
(Staring up at the painting)

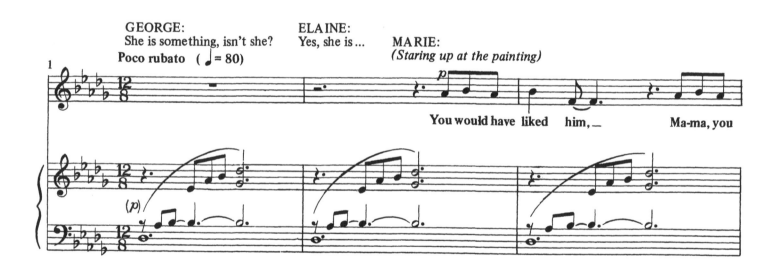

You would have liked him, —

Ma-ma, you

would. Ma-ma, he makes things -- Ma-ma, they're good.

No. 31

AFTER CHILDREN

(fade)

No. 32   LESSON #8
(GEORGE)

DENNIS: George. I look forward to seeing
          what you come up with next.

GEORGE: *(Smiling)* You're not the only one, Dennis. *(Dennis exits)*

41

G.

Stretch-ing his vi -sion in ev-'ry di - rec - tion.____ See George at-temp-ting to see a   con-

44

nec-tion ____ When all he can   see _____ Is may-be a

48

(Humorously)

tree -- _____ The fam - i - ly   tree -- _____ Sor - ry, Ma -

52

rie ...

No. 33

MOVE ON
(GEORGE, DOT)

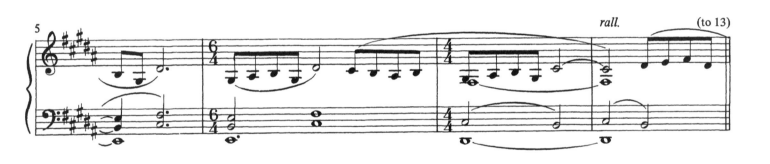

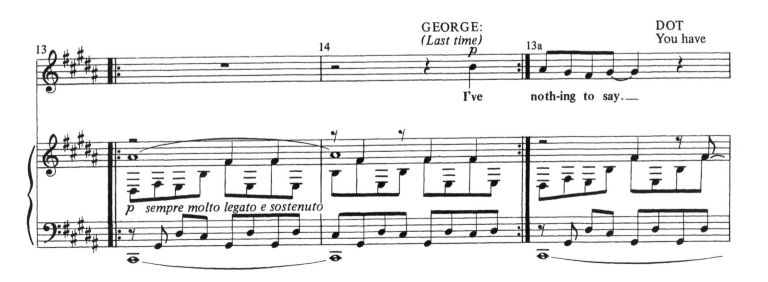

220

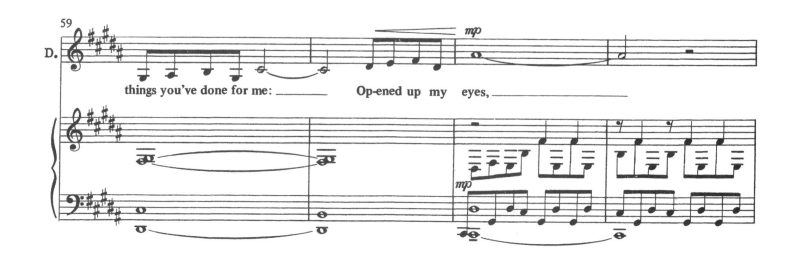

things you've done for me: _____ Op-ened up my eyes, _____

Taught me how to see,

No-tice ev-'ry tree ... Un-der-stand the

GEORGE:

...No-tice ev-'ry tree...

us - ual - ly do. _____ You keep mov-ing on. _____

dim.

Poco animato

Look at what you've done, Then at what you want, Not at where you are, What you'll

GEORGE: *(Looking around)*

...Some-thing in the light, Some-thing in the sky, In the grass, Up be-

234

No. 34

SUNDAY — FINALE
(COMPANY)

ALL MEN:

On the green____ Or-ange vi - o - let mass   Of the grass

ALL WOMEN:

Of the grass

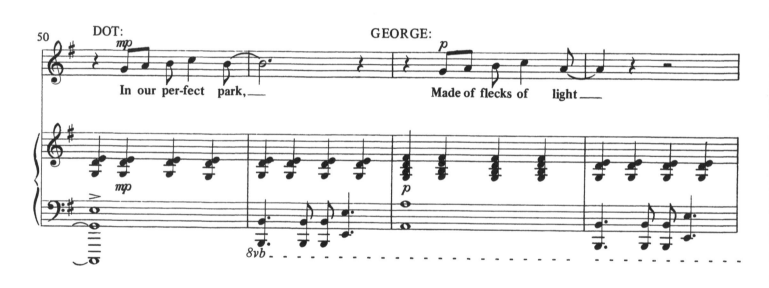

DOT:

In our per-fect park,____

GEORGE:

Made of flecks of light____

And dark,____   And   par - a - sols:_____

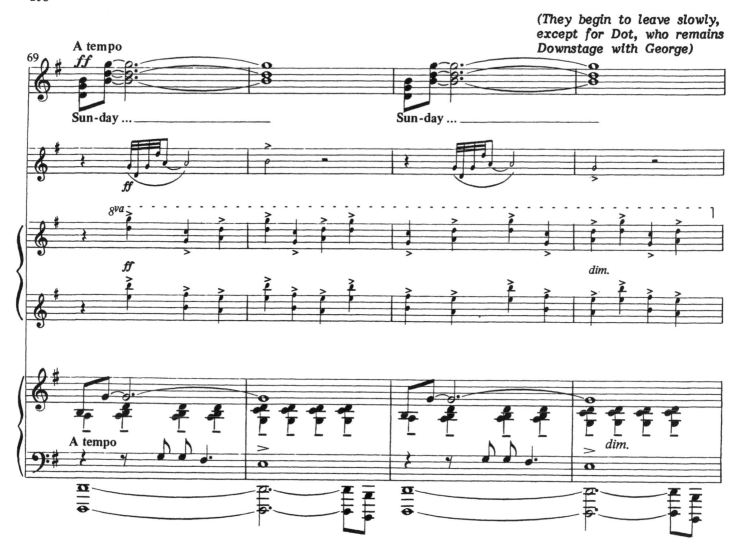

(They begin to leave slowly,
except for Dot, who remains
Downstage with George)

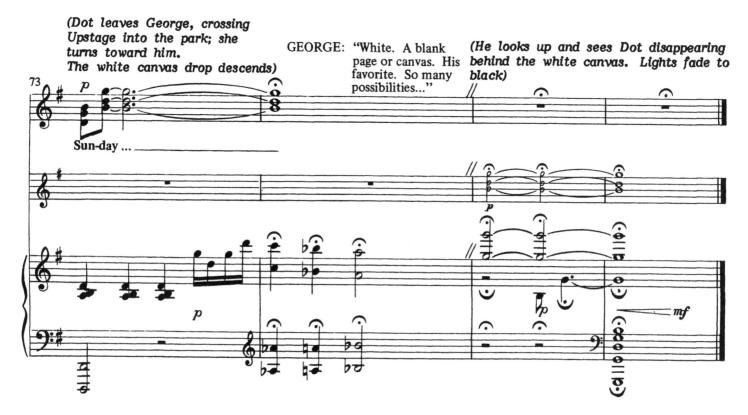

(Dot leaves George, crossing
Upstage into the park; she
turns toward him.
The white canvas drop descends)

GEORGE: "White. A blank
page or canvas. His
favorite. So many
possibilities..."

(He looks up and sees Dot disappearing
behind the white canvas. Lights fade to
black)

End of Act II

No. 35   BOWS

19

(Dot and George's bows)

22

244

rall.
(2nd time only)

After 2nd time, segue

No. 36

EXIT MUSIC